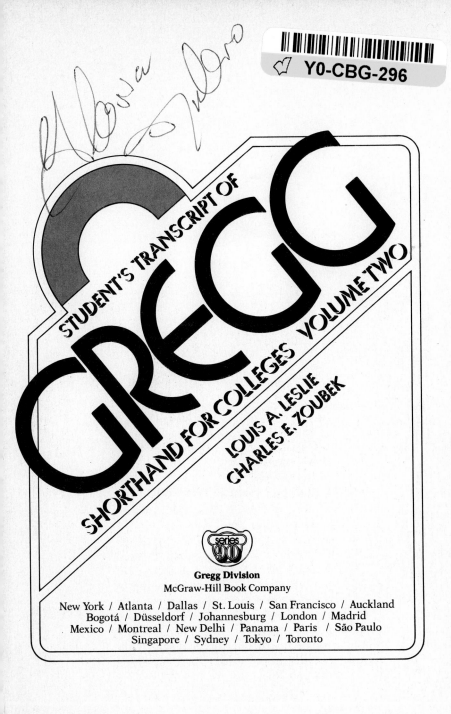

STUDENT'S TRANSCRIPT OF

GREGG

SHORTHAND FOR COLLEGES · VOLUME TWO

LOUIS A. LESLIE
CHARLES E. ZOUBEK

series 90

Gregg Division
McGraw-Hill Book Company

New York / Atlanta / Dallas / St. Louis / San Francisco / Auckland
Bogotá / Düsseldorf / Johannesburg / London / Madrid
Mexico / Montreal / New Delhi / Panama / Paris / São Paulo
Singapore / Sydney / Tokyo / Toronto

5 6 7 8 9 0 DODO 8 8 7 6 5 4

ISBN 0-07-037755-3

Explanation to Users of This Booklet

This booklet contains the transcript to the shorthand material in the Reading and Writing Practice exercises of *Greeg Shorthand for Colleges, Volume Two, Series 90*. The number preceding each exercise corresponds to the shorthand exercise number in the text. This transcript will serve two desirable purposes:

1 It will enable the students to look up the word or phrase represented by any outline about which they are in doubt. They will thus be able to cover the Reading and Writing Practice exercises more quickly and with a minimum of discouragement.

2 Because the key material is counted, the students will be able to obtain extra dictation practice outside of class.

The Publishers

Transcript of Shorthand

(The material is counted in groups of 20 standard words, or 28 syllables, for convenience in timing the reading or dictation.)

CHAPTER 1

LESSON 1

3 Dear Mr. Smith: Our organization is happy to announce the addition of General clothing to our[1] line of fine wearing apparel. We now have the largest, most complete selection of clothing of any wholesale[2] dealer in the entire area.

General clothes are very popular throughout the nation. They have been[3] among the best-sellers in the nation for several years, and they will probably be one of our best-sellers as well.[4]

We are sending you a complete listing of all General clothing that we will be carrying. Take a few[5] moments, Mr. Smith, to let us know which particular things you would like to add to your line. Cordially yours, [118]

4 Dear Miss White: Recently I visited your store, the General Shoe Shop. I picked out a nice pair of shoes, paid cash[1] for them, and asked that they be mailed to my home.

The shoes had not arrived after several days, and I returned to the[2] store. I discovered that the delivery company had picked up the package but had somehow misplaced it. The[3] clerk gave me another pair of shoes, and I took them home with me. This morning, however, I received a bill in[4] the mail.

I am sure there is some mistake, but I want to be sure that this charge is deleted from your records. Please[5] take care of this transaction as soon as possible. I hope you will call me immediately if you have[6] any questions. Sincerely yours, [125]

5 Dear Ms. Green: Thank you very much for writing to **me** about the problem you experienced with the shoes you recently bought from our store.[1]

The shoes were indeed misplaced during delivery. I am very glad that you were[2] able to get another pair exactly like the first when you returned to the store.

The bill you received was sent to[3] you in error, of course. Please disregard this bill and be assured that your account shows a zero balance.

We[4] appreciate your business, Ms. Green, and we hope you will visit our store regularly in the future. Very[5] sincerely yours, [102]

6 Dear Mr. Hale: In December I had the pleasure of hearing you make a short presentation to the Dallas[1] Publishing Association on the subject of metrics in the publishing business. I was very much[2] impressed with the talk, and I would like to ask you to make a similar presentation to my association,[3] the Troy Publishing Club, at its regular spring meeting in April. The presentation can be made on April[4] 3, 4, or 5.

I understand that your talks are usually sponsored by the General Electronics Company[5] and that your speaking schedule is arranged by them. I trust you will forward this request to them.

I certainly[6] hope that you will be able to accept this invitation to speak to our organization. We will be looking[7] forward to hearing from you soon. Cordially yours, [150]

7 Dear Miss Bates: Thank you for your letter inviting me to speak at the regular spring meeting of the Troy Publishing[1] Club in April. I wish that it were possible for me to come to Troy, but I will be out of the state on[2] a business trip during the entire month of April.

I will be available if you would like me to come in[3] May, June, or July. If you need someone to speak on the metric system in April, however, I would like to[4] suggest Ms. Mary Jones of the General Business College. She is one of the leading authorities on the[5] subject, and she would be available to speak to your group on April 3, 4, or 5.

Please call me if I can[6] be of help to you in the future. Yours very sincerely, [131]

8 Dear Sir or Madam: I was in Chicago on a trip last month, and I bought a small lamp in your department store.[1] It was a beautiful green lamp that I purchased as a gift for a good friend. I ordi-

narily check to see[2] if electrical appliances work satisfactorily before I leave the store. On that day, however,[3] I was in a hurry, and I did not check the lamp. I discovered that it would not work after I returned to[4] my home.

Please let me know if I should send the lamp back to you or have it repaired here. I am enclosing a copy[5] of the sales slip. Yours truly, [106]

9 Dear Mr. Gold: I am very glad you found a lamp that you liked well enough to purchase as a gift for a[1] good friend when you were in our store last month. I am, of course, very sorry that the lamp did not work satisfactorily[2] when you returned home. The fault is entirely ours. We should have checked it carefully before we sold it to[3] you. We usually make inspections like this as a matter of routine. This time we failed to do so.

You may have[4] the lamp repaired, and we will reimburse you for the bill. You may mail the lamp back to us for repair or for a[5] refund if you prefer.

We will be very happy to take care of the matter immediately when we hear[6] from you. Sincerely yours, [124]

LESSON 2

5 Dear Mrs. Moore: We are happy to tell you about the opening of our conveniently located new toy[1] store in the Boston Shopping Center. In our new store you will find the largest stock of toys in the state. We have toys[2] that will appeal to everyone. We have safe toys for very young children. We have educational toys for[3] students. We have mechanical toys and games that will appeal to both children and adults.

All our toys and games are of[4] the best construction. Stop in to see us the next time you want to buy toys or games for your children, your friends, or[5] yourself. Yours truly, [104]

6 Dear Miss Smith: You will recall that several weeks ago I bought a new sweater for my niece, Jane Green, in the clothing[1] department of your store in Philadelphia. It is a beautiful sweater, and it was quite expensive. My[2] niece was very happy with the sweater until today. She had taken it to the dry cleaners yesterday, and[3] today she returned to pick it up.

The sweater looked very nice except for the trim. The color had faded[4] badly, and it made the garment look old. I would like, therefore, to return the sweater for a full refund. May I do[5] so? Yours truly, [103]

7 Dear Mr. Allen: We are pleased to announce the opening of our new office furniture store in the Miami[1] Shopping Center in your neighborhood. Our new store is the largest, most complete office furniture shop in this[2] part of the state.

We have every type of office chair available on the market today. There are swivel chairs,[3] posture chairs, and executive chairs. They come in either wood or metal.

You will also find in our store a wide[4] range of office desks in all sizes. We have desks designed to fit in small places and desks that will complement the[5] most elegant executive suite.

Come to our convenient new store for all your furniture needs. We are open[6] every day except Sunday. Yours very truly, [130]

8 Dear Mrs. Tate: In January we moved our company offices to Indiana. About that time we[1] purchased a large conference table from your office furniture store in Indianapolis. We wanted to[2] use it in the board room of our organization.

The table is well designed, and the construction is quite sturdy.[3] The table is very beautiful, but it has not been serviceable. We placed the table in a room that is[4] much too small. We should have realized that the table would not fit in this room before we purchased it, but we did not.[5]

We now find that we must replace it with one that is smaller. May we return this table to you either as a[6] trade-in on a new one or for a refund? I hope to hear from you soon. Sincerely yours, [136]

9 Dear Mr. Murphy: Thank you for writing to me about the conference table you purchased from our store in[1] Indianapolis. We received your letter in the mail this morning. Under ordinary circumstances we would[2] be very glad to take back any product that is not satisfactory. In this case, how-

ever, we cannot.[3]

You will remember that you purchased the table during a special sale at our store. All the items that were sold[4] at that time were things we had obtained from the Minneapolis Office Supply Company. That company had[5] suffered severe business reverses, and we bought most of their stock at a liquidation sale. We then sold this[6] furniture to the public at very low prices.

We are sorry about this, Mr. Murphy, but I am sure you[7] can understand our position. Sincerely yours, [149]

10 Dear Mr. James: On Monday, October 23, the St. Paul Department Store will have one of the biggest sales[1] in its history. There will be wonderful bargains available in every department in the store.

In the[2] furniture department you will be able to take advantage of low prices on sofas, chairs, and tables. In[3] the clothing department you will be able to save on coats, suits, and hats. In the glass department you can take[4] away great buys on single items or complete sets of dishes.

Make your plans to be with us October 23[5] for the biggest and best sale in our history. Sincerely yours, [112]

11 Dear Mrs. Carson: On Monday, October 23, you will be able to make savings that you probably[1] thought were not possible. On that date the St. Paul Department Store will hold its annual sale of fine clothing. You[2] will be

able to find great savings on such items as dresses, coats, and leisure suits. You will, in addition, be[3] able to make big savings on shoes of every type and style.

Mark October 23 on your calendar now.[4] We will be looking forward to seeing you in our store on that date. Sincerely yours, [95]

LESSON 3

4 Dear Mr. Chase: The General Clothing Store is closing its doors. It is with regret that we announce our closing[1] after many years of service to the people of Des Moines.

Why have we decided to take this action? The[2] answer is simple. We lost our lease, and we have not been able to find another building in the area with[3] ample space for our operation.

What does this mean to you? It means that customers can make wonderful savings[4] on all their purchases for the next few weeks. You will be able to save money on suits, coats, and shoes. Come in[5] any day during August, Mr. Chase, and select the items you need to complete your wardrobe. You may never[6] again be able to enjoy such great savings.

It has been a pleasure serving the people of Des Moines, and we will[7] miss being a part of the business community. Sincerely yours, [153]

5 Dear Customer: The General Factory Outlet will open its doors for business in September, and we are[1] now looking for people to work in our beautiful new store.

We have openings for salespeople, accountants, and[2] stock clerks. No previous experience is necessary for most of the positions.

Enclosed is an[3] application blank for you to use if you wish to apply for a position with us. Simply fill it out, sign it, and[4] return it to us. We will schedule a personal interview for you as soon as we receive your application.[5] Sincerely yours,   [104]

6 Dear Miss Case: It was a pleasure to receive your application for a National credit card in the mail[1] today. Thank you for choosing our company as your source for convenient, easy shopping.

We are now processing your[2] application, and we should have our work completed within a week or so. You will receive your card just as soon[3] as we have finished our work.

We know, Miss Case, that you will enjoy using your new National credit card when it[4] arrives. It is accepted by most major department stores in every large city throughout the country. We look[5] forward to serving you for many years to come. Sincerely yours,   [112]

7 Dear Mrs. Green: It is a pleasure to announce that the Brown Factory Outlet has added Hamilton pottery,[1] glass, and other dishes to our line of fine products. We are able to offer Hamilton dishes to you[2] at discount prices through a special arrangement with the Hamilton factory.

You probably know that Hamilton[3] is the largest manufacturer of glass products in the entire area. Enclosed is a booklet[4] showing all of the beautiful new pieces that we now carry in open stock. We are sure you will agree with us[5] that Hamilton dishes are among the finest, most beautiful in the world.

Plan to come in soon and let one of[6] our representatives show you the complete line of Hamilton products. We will give you one free cup, plate, or[7] other piece of Hamilton pottery when you visit our store. Cordially yours,   [154]

8 Dear Miss Case: Enclosed is your new National credit card. Welcome, Miss Case, to our large family of National[1] credit card holders.

Please take a moment right now to sign your credit card in ink. It would be a very good[2] idea for you to record the number of the card in your personal file. Be sure to carry your credit card with[3] you at all times. Please notify us immediately if your card should ever be lost or stolen.

People all[4] over the country use their National credit cards to purchase everything from towels to television sets.[5] You will find that the card is accepted by stores throughout the country. You will also discover that it is a[6] valuable form of identification when you want to cash a personal check.

Thank you for your confidence[7] in our organization. Welcome to the largest group of credit card holders in the world. Cordially yours,   [159]

9 Dear Miss Garcia: Thank you for your recent request for a General credit card. We were, of course, very glad[1] to receive your request.

We are now in the process of making our regular credit check, and we will send you[2] your card just as soon as we have completed our work.

In the meantime, Miss Garcia, we are sending you our new[3] catalog. I hope you will enjoy looking through it. When you receive your credit card, you may charge any item[4] in the catalog. Sincerely yours, [87]

10 Dear Miss Washington: It was a pleasure meeting you last week when I came to your office for an interview. I[1] was very much impressed with your sales organization and with the way you manage your office. I am more[2] convinced than ever that Smith and Company is the place where I should work.

I have asked several people to write character[3] and business references for me. I am sure you will be receiving these letters soon.

I hope, Miss Washington,[4] that you will decide to give me an opportunity to prove myself with your company. I am eager to[5] work, and I assure you I can do a very good job for you. Cordially yours, [114]

LESSON 4

4 Dear Miss Simon: Recently I was in Miami and purchased a new leather chair at your furniture store. It[1] was to have been delivered to me yesterday at my home in Orlando. I waited for several hours, but[2] the delivery truck never arrived.

I have been purchasing furniture at your store for many years, and I[3] know that your firm is usually reliable and dependable. I am, of course, quite disappointed with your[4] service in this instance.

I hope you will check into this matter and let me know what caused the trouble. Please also[5] let me know when you can give me a definite delivery date. Sincerely yours, [115]

5 Gentlemen: Last week on a brief visit to Philadelphia I bought a suede jacket from your leather goods store.[1] I noticed that there was a slight imperfection in the jacket when I returned to my home in Boston. One of[2] the sleeves is of a lighter color than the other.

I would like to return the coat to your store for a full[3] refund. Please advise me where you wish the coat sent and when I may expect to receive a refund check. Very truly[4] yours, [81]

6 Dear Mr. Mason: Thank you for advising me of the problem you are having with the suede jacket you[1] recently bought at the Huntington Leather Goods Shop. We are indeed sorry that the color of one of the sleeves appears[2] to be somewhat lighter than the other.

I hope you will take another close look at the coat before you return[3] it. It is a characteristic of suede to appear different under varying degrees of light. The grain of[4] the leather can make it seem to change color almost before your eyes.

We believe that you will probably want to[5] keep the coat. Should you decide to return it, however, just pack it carefully, insure it, and mail it back to[6] us. We will cheerfully refund the full purchase price. Very sincerely yours,   [134]

7 Dear Ms. Brown: Here is some good advice for you. Stop in the new Huntington Leather Goods Shop the next time you are in[1] the market for leather goods. There you will find beautiful new leather jackets, coats, and shoes.

We are sure you will be[2] pleased with our line of goods and with our reasonable prices. Our beautiful showroom is open Monday through[3] Saturday. We are closed on Sunday.

We are offering new customers a special discount on their first purchase at[4] the Huntington Leather Goods Shop. Just bring this letter with you and show it to our sales representative when you[5] make your first purchase. You will receive a special discount on the regular price. We will be looking forward to[6] seeing you in our shop soon. Sincerely yours,   [128]

8 Dear Miss Garcia: Our organization, the Jennings Furniture Company, does not usually give advice,[1] but in this case we are making an exception. We advise you to come to our store as quickly as possible.[2] What is the reason

for this advice? It is simple. We are having the sale of a lifetime.

You will be able[3] to make great savings on practically every item we sell during the next week. We have beautiful new[4] furniture for your living room, your bedroom, and your kitchen. We can supply just the items you need at prices that[5] are unbeatable.

Take our advice, Miss Garcia. Come to the Jennings Furniture Company today. You will[6] be making no mistake. Sincerely yours,   [127]

9 Dear Mr. Yale: Last week I purchased a new Superior refrigerator at your furniture store on Main[1] Street in Birmingham. I paid for it with a check. The refrigerator was scheduled for delivery yesterday.[2]

The truck arrived right on time, and the appliance was the one I selected. It was placed in the kitchen, but[3] there was a problem. Neither the motor nor the light would work. I had to refuse the refrigerator, of course.[4] The delivery people politely took it back to your store.

Now I am wondering, Mr. Yale, what I ought[5] to do. Will you send another appliance, or will you credit my account for the price I paid? Please advise me[6] as soon as possible. Sincerely yours, [127]

10 Dear Miss Lee: Thank you for writing to us about the problem you had with the new refrigerator you recently[1] purchased from our store. We are, of course, very sorry that you have had trouble. The refrigerator you chose[2] is usu-

ally one of our most efficient, dependable models.

I am sorry to advise you, Miss Lee,[3] that we do not have another refrigerator exactly like the one you chose. I hope you choose another[4] model soon. We will give you a special discount if you should choose a more expensive model.

Please let us hear from[5] you soon. Sincerely yours, [104]

LESSON 5

3 *The Art of Selling*

Over the years the job of selling goods and services has progressed to what some people call[1] an art. You will probably know what these people mean if you have recently had the good fortune to purchase[2] something from a professional sales representative. You may, on the other hand, have recently had the misfortune[3] of dealing with a poorly prepared, surly sales representative. In this case you will probably take[4] objection to the idea that selling is an art.

At one time or other we have all found ourselves in the[5] position of trying to purchase goods from a person who did not know much about the product. This, of course, can be[6] very frustrating. Some time ago a man walked into a tire store and asked the sales representative to[7] describe the advantages and disadvantages of radial tires. The representative was a young man who[8] had not been on the job very long. It would have been better if he had asked for

help from an experienced[9] person, but he chose not to do so. He quickly opened a pamphlet and tried to find the answers to the questions. The[10] customer wanted to know how strong the tires were, how long they could be expected to last, and if they were guaranteed.[11] The sales representative could give answers to none of these questions.

The customer became impatient and[12] left the store in anger. He promptly went to another tire store across the street and made a purchase. The young sales[13] representative learned the hard way that having product knowledge is a vital part of the job of selling.

A[14] woman recently entered a large department store and asked the first employee that she saw where she could find the[15] furniture department. The employee was a woman who had worked a long time in the shoe department, and she[16] simply pointed to the escalator without saying a word. The customer asked another employee in[17] the shirt department for more specific directions. The man seemed irritated and told the customer to check[18] the directory located at the entrance to the building. The customer was frankly disgusted by this[19] time and left the store.

Neither of these two employees seemed to care. Their attitude was that the customer would have[20] to find the furniture department by herself because she was not interested in purchasing anything[21] from their particular departments. What they did not realize was that their surly attitude created a[22] very bad image for the entire company. The woman probably did not return to the store to buy any[23] items at all. An attitude of service would have gone a long way to helping the store keep the woman as a[24] customer.

Some stores operate on a commission basis. This means that the sales representatives are paid a[25] percentage of the price of anything they sell. In some cases the representatives become very aggressive[26] and try to push goods that the customer really does not want or need. A clever sales representative can[27] sometimes actually sell a customer many things that the customer did not intend to buy. This,[28] however, does not create goodwill for the store in the long run.

A few years ago a potential customer named Frank[29] Strong made a long trip from the suburbs to Boston to purchase a new car. Although his present car was not really[30] old, it had never performed the way he wanted it to. He actually felt that the car was beyond repair.[31] The sales representative could easily have sold Mr. Strong a car at that time. However, it was obvious[32] to the representative that the car was actually in very good condition and could be repaired[33] easily and quickly by the proper mechanic. The sales representative introduced Mr. Strong to the[34] head of the repair department in the agency, and in only a few hours, the car was running perfectly.[35] Did this lose a customer for the automobile agency? It certainly did not. In fact, it actually[36] created a very good customer for the future. Mr. Strong has purchased two new cars from the agency[37] since that time and swears that he will buy all his cars there in the future.

A lesson can be learned about the art of[38] selling through the preceding examples. The good sales representative must be willing to give prompt service to[39] each customer. This is true whether or not the customer actually buys something from that particular[40] representative. A good sales representative must have a friendly, helpful attitude. The goodwill[41] generated by this kind of attitude lasts in the mind of the customer for a long time. The sales representative[42] must know everything possible about the product in order to give the customer adequate,[43] reliable information.

A salesperson can turn the job of selling into the art of selling simply by[44] observing these simple rules.   [885]

CHAPTER 2

LESSON 6

3 Dear Executive: Are you one of a large number of business executives in this country who are not good[1] public speakers? Have you tried time and again to improve your speaking ability to little avail?

If you[2] have, the General School of Public Speaking would like to tell you what we can do for you in as little as a[3] month to help you improve your speaking ability.

A short course at the General School of Public Speaking[4] provides you with special instruction in planning and organizing talks. In addition, it gives you the opportunity[5] to practice speaking before other business executives who are also working to improve themselves.[6]

The cost is small, but the returns are big. Take advantage of this opportunity without delay. Write us[7] today for further information. Cordially yours,   [149]

4 Dear Mr. Morris: If you are planning to enter the business world after graduation from high school, why not[1] give yourself the advantage of a good technical education by spending a few short months at Jones Technical[2] Institute. At our school you will be able to choose from a number of interesting, exciting technical[3] fields. We have courses in data processing, electronics, and mechanical drawing.

Enclosed is a brochure[4] that tells about several of the many interesting courses we offer. Take a few minutes now to look at the[5] brochure. If you would like to have further information, just call us. Cordially yours,   [115]

5 Dear Miss Kent: During our regular check of credits for students who are planning to graduate in June, we found[1] a minor problem in your records. There is a discrepancy between your transcript of credits from Smith College[2] and your State College degree plan.

When you transferred from Smith College to State College last year, there were courses in[3] public speaking and business correspondence for which you were not given credit. Your transcript from Smith College shows that[4] you enrolled in the courses, but there are no final grades. In all probability these were courses that you[5] completed after the transcript was mailed.

If you have completed these courses, please have Smith College send us a current[6] transcript so that we will be able to process your papers for graduation. Cordially yours,   [137]

6 Gentlemen: Last year I transferred from Smith College to State College in order to pursue a course of study in[1] advertising. At that time I asked that a complete transcript of my credits be mailed to State College.

Apparently[2] there is an error in your records. The transcript shows no final grades in my courses in public speaking and[3] business correspondence. Frankly, I am quite concerned. If you will call the teachers involved, I am sure they will[4] verify the fact that I did actually complete these courses.

Because my graduation depends on the prompt[5] resolution of this problem, I hope that you will take care of the problem immediately. Sincerely yours,[6]   [120]

7 Dear Miss Kent: Enclosed is a copy of your current transcript. I am sure you will be glad to note that the incomplete[1] grades in public speaking and business correspondence have been cleared. Dr. Jane Mills, the head of the department,[2] has verified that you did indeed complete these courses.

We have mailed the registrar of State College a new[3] transcript showing the changes. If we can be of further assistance to you, please let us know. Sincerely yours, [77]

8 Dear Mr. Jones: Thank you very much for your recent letter concerning the advantages of attending Jones[1] Technical Institute. Thank you also for the brochure that you sent describing the various courses that you[2] offer.

Next month I will be graduating from high school, and I definitely plan to further my education.[3] However, I do not wish to spend many years in college before I begin working. I want to obtain a[4] job as soon as possible and continue school in the evenings.

Please send me a complete catalog listing all[5] the courses that you offer and the times at which I may take them. I am, of course, basically interested in night[6] courses, but I might be able to take one or two courses in the daytime if my work will permit.

I would also[7] like for one of your counselors to visit me at my home to discuss my attending Jones Technical[8] Institute. I am at home in the evenings on weekdays and on Sundays in the afternoon. Thank you for your[9] consideration, Mr. Jones. I am looking forward to receiving more information about your school in the near[10] future. Sincerely yours, [204]

9 Dear Mrs. James: Thank you very much, Mrs. James, for sending me a copy of the complete transcript from Smith College.[1] Thank you also for sending a copy to the registrar here at State College. With your help I have been able[2] to complete the preliminary work in applying for my degree in advertising. If all goes well,[3] the degree will be granted in June.

I am planning to continue my formal education after graduation[4] from State College, and I would like to have information about the graduate programs at Smith College.[5] If you have a catalog of graduate courses, please send me a copy at your convenience. Sincerely yours,[6] [120]

LESSON 7

5 Dear Miss Lee: Because you will soon be graduating from high school, you are probably thinking about what you will[1] be doing in the future. Every year many young men and women make the decision to attend a business[2] college for a year or so and then take a promising job in business.

If you want to attend business college[3] after graduation, you need travel no farther than Dallas. We invite you to consider Dallas Business[4] College, one of the finest schools of its type in the entire area. Dallas Business College is accredited[5] and offers a wide variety of programs designed to fit your personal needs. We have special areas[6] of study in secretarial science, management, and accounting. One of these fields will probably be[7] just the one you are looking for.

If you will fill out and return the enclosed card, we will have one of our[8] representatives come to visit you in your home to give you further information.

We hope to have you as a[9] student soon. Very cordially yours, [186]

6 Dear Mrs. Cook: It was a wonderful experience for me to be able to work with you for the past few[1] months as a student teacher at West Phoenix High School. I feel that I learned a great deal every day, and this was a[2] direct result of your concern and consideration for me. You are indeed a professional person, and[3] my goal is to become a teacher who is as efficient and dedicated as you.

As you know, I will be[4] graduating from college in a few weeks, and I plan to submit my application for a teaching position[5] to several schools after that time. I would appreciate it, Mrs. Cook, if you would consent to serve as a[6] reference for me.

Thanks for your wonderful help during the past school term. Cordially yours, [135]

7 Dear Mr. Marks: Your very nice letter arrived today. Thank you very much for your complimentary remarks[1] about my teaching ability.

It was a pleasure to help you with your student teaching during the past term.[2] You progressed very fast, and I have confidence that you will be an excellent teacher.

This morning Miss Ellen[3] Brand, the principal of Denver Central High School, called me. One of her teachers will be leaving Colorado[4] after the first of the year, and she needs a replacement. She asked me if I could recommend a good person for the[5] position. Of course, I gave her your name. I am sure you will be hearing from her in a few days.

I will, of course,[6] give you a good recommendation at any school to which you apply. When you accept a position, please let[7] me know where you will be teaching next year. Very sincerely yours, [152]

8 Dear Mr. Jenkins: For the past few months I have been teaching in the evening school of Brown High School here in Georgia[1]. In the school we have a number of students who have recently come here from foreign countries. There are students from[2] Spain, France, and Germany. Some come from countries that are even farther away.

These students are usually adults[3] who have limited basic skills and who wish to learn to read and write English. I have had some trouble finding the[4] kind of materials I need to teach the students. The main problem is that some of the students need elementary[5] reading books while others need somewhat more advanced books. However, all the students need interesting,[6] informative material.

If your company publishes books or magazines that I could use in my class, I[7] would certainly appreciate receiving sample copies so that I can evaluate them. Yours truly, [158]

9 Dear Ms. Gray: Thank you for your inquiry about our textbooks for teaching English to foreign students. We are[1] happy to send you our complete catalog of materials. I am sure you will agree with us that you need look[2] no further. We have all the materials you need for your class.

Please pay particular attention to the books[3] on basic skills. This series of books has been specifically designed for classes such as yours. There are basic[4] readers, spellers, and language books. Each of them contains interesting, informative stories and articles. In[5] addition, there are books on the intermediate and advanced levels with similar content.

If you would like[6] to review some of the books described in the catalog, just fill out the enclosed form and return it to us at[7] our Alabama office. We will be happy to send you review copies for your consideration. Sincerely[8] yours, [161]

LESSON 8

4 Dear Friend: Several years ago the Portland school board called for a bond election to provide funds to build a new sports[1] stadium for the public schools. At that time the city faced many financial problems, and there was a great deal[2] of opposition to any increase in taxes. The bond issue was defeated by a narrow margin.[3]

Portland is now in better financial condition, and the school board has called another bond election to try once[4] again to get the approval of the voters. We need the assistance of every voter in the city. I[5] hope you will give the matter a great deal of consideration and cast your ballot in favor of the bond[6] issue this year.

The young people of the city are depending on you. It will give them a facility of[7] unmatched excellence, and it will be a great asset to Portland. Sincerely yours, [154]

5 Dear Friends: The Portland school board is calling a bond election in October to finance a new sports stadium[1] for the public schools. I am sure you are aware of the need for a new stadium in the city. The old one[2] was built many years ago and is badly in need of repair. Unfortunately, we would have to spend more to[3] repair the old stadium than it would cost to build a new one.

It seems that the logical thing to do is to[4] construct a new facility. The school board has chosen a new site near the interstate highway that seems to be[5] the best place for a new stadium.

The young people of our city deserve your confidence and your assistance.[6] Please give your support to help them obtain this new facility. Vote for the bond issue in October. Very[7] cordially yours, [143]

6 Dear Mr. Porter: As you know, the school board is calling a special election to attempt to finance the[1] construction of a new stadium for the public schools.

I am sure you will remember that several years ago a[2] similar bond issue was called. At that time the issue was soundly defeated. The people clearly showed their[3] preference to repair the old stadium rather than to build a new one. The principal reason for the defeat[4] was the large increase in taxes that would have resulted from the issuance of the bonds. The same problem exists[5] today. Every resident of Portland will face a large increase in taxes if the issue is passed.

Most of the[6] citizens of our city believe that the old stadium can be renovated at a small fraction of the[7] cost of building a new one. Please join the group of people who are vitally interested in keeping the cost[8] of running our local schools at the least possible amount while furnishing quality education for our[9] youth. Vote no in the upcoming bond election. Yours truly,   [191]

7 Dear Miss Kenny: Because I have maintained a residence in Salt Lake City for many years, I am in a good[1] position to know the special needs of our city. Because I was a teacher at Utah College for many[2] years, I am in a particularly good position to know the educational needs of our students. As[3] a voter, you are in the position to help elect me to the Utah Board of Regents in the election[4] to be held next month.

My background in teaching management, finance, and accounting and my dedication to[5] education make me the best choice for the position. I am an independent candidate and am not[6] aligned with any political party in the state. Please help me and your state by casting your ballot for me in[7] the upcoming election. Very truly yours,   [149]

8 Dear Mr. Lopez: I want to take this opportunity to thank you for the wonderful assistance and support[1] that you gave me during the recent political campaign. As you know, I was not successful in winning[2] a seat on the school board, but I feel that my efforts were well spent.

The goodwill that was created during the campaign[3] has given me the confidence to run for office again next year. In fact, I am already beginning[4] to lay the groundwork for the next election. I hope, Mr. Lopez, that you will again serve on my election[5] committee.

If you are interested in working with me again, please let me know as soon as possible. If[6] we begin work soon, I am confident that I can win the next election. Sincerely yours,   [137]

9 Dear Voter: As I am sure you realize, the Ft. Worth school board election will take place on Thursday, May 21.[1] There are several candidates running for the positions that are open.

Each of the candidates is well[2] qualified, but you must decide for yourself who is best qualified. The

League of Voters has prepared the enclosed pamphlet[3] giving a brief history on each of the candidates. Take a few minutes to study the pamphlet carefully.[4]

On May 21 take time to cast your ballot for those candidates who you feel are best qualified for the job.[5] Your city and your schools depend on your good judgment. Very sincerely yours, [114]

LESSON 9

4 Dear Mr. Edwards: The citizens of our city will soon be asked to approve bonds to construct several new[1] elementary schools throughout the city. As you may know, one of the schools is planned for our neighborhood. The residents[2] of this area need a new school very much.

During the past decade the population in our neighborhood[3] has increased greatly. There is only one school in the entire area, and it is badly overcrowded.[4] We hope you will give your full support to this bond issue by asking all your friends to vote for it and by voting[5] for it yourself.

If you would like some illustrated leaflets outlining the tentative plans for the buildings, just[6] let me know. I will be very happy to supply you with them. Sincerely yours, [134]

5 Dear Miss Cunningham: Thank you very much for your letter telling me of your support for the upcoming bond[1] issue to finance construction of several elementary schools in neighborhoods throughout the city. I have gone[2] over the plans backwards and forwards, and I believe that construction of each of the schools is justified. I want[3] you to know, Miss Cunningham, that I intend to vote for the issue and will encourage my friends to do so.

If[4] you are planning any meetings to disseminate information about the need for new school buildings, I hope[5] you will invite me to attend. Sincerely yours, [109]

6 Dear Friend: As you are aware, a school bond issue has been called for next month to finance the construction of several[1] new elementary schools. Outwardly, the proposal seems to be a very good one. Most of the schools should be[2] built. However, some of the schools are to be constructed in areas where the population is actually[3] decreasing.

Obviously, the need for new schools is not the same in each of the many neighborhoods of the city.[4] However, the way the current proposal reads, the money will be divided equally among the various[5] neighborhoods.

A group of concerned citizens believes that the construction of certain schools would be a waste of money.[6] Unfortunately, there is only one question on the ballot. If you vote for any part of the package, you[7] must vote for all of it. As a result, we feel compelled to ask the citizens to vote no on the complete[8] package. Between now and election day we will be making a concerted effort to have the issue defeated.[9] In this way we believe we can get the school board to call another bond issue in the near future to finance[10] only those schools that are actually needed.

Help keep our city from wasting money on unneeded school facilities.[11] Vote no in the upcoming election. Yours truly, [231]

7 Dear Mrs. Lexington: As I am sure you are aware, there has been a great deal of opposition to the school[1] bond issue that has been called for next month. The main problem seems to be that there is only one item on the[2] ballot. The citizens must vote either for or against the complete package.

While about half the voters seem to[3] approve the construction of schools, there is resistance to the construction of schools in neighborhoods where the population[4] is decreasing. Sentiment seems to be divided equally between the two factions. Therefore, there is great[5] danger that the issue will fail.

I believe, Mrs. Lexington, that the school board must compromise by putting each[6] item on the ballot separately. In that way the voters will have an opportunity to vote for one or[7] more of the items without having to approve the complete plan. This seems to be the only way that any of[8] the items will be approved. Sincerely yours, [168]

8 Dear Mr. Washington: As you know, last month the citizens of our city voted to construct a new[1] elementary school that will be lo-

cated in your neighborhood. We have asked a local architect to begin work[2] on the plans for the school. However, we want the residents of the neighborhood to be involved in the initial[3] planning of the building. We feel that the input of the parents, students, and other residents of the[4] area will definitely help us to plan the type of school that will be of greatest value to all concerned.

In[5] the next week or so we will announce the time and date of an open meeting at which everyone in the immediate[6] area may express opinions and give advice about the type of school that should be constructed in[7] the neighborhood. We want to know if there is a need for an auditorium in the school or if the residents[8] would rather have a gymnasium that could be used for assemblies as well as sporting events. We also[9] need to know if the people in the area would like to have a library that could be used by everyone[10] in the community.

Please watch the local newspapers, Mr. Washington, for the announcement. Then plan to be[11] with us to let us know just the type of school facility that you believe would be of greatest value to the[12] students in your area. We will certainly appreciate your support in this matter. Very cordially[13] yours, [261]

9 Ladies and Gentlemen: It is with a great deal of pleasure that the school board announces the opening of Smith[1] Elementary School. Classes will actually begin

in September, but we wish to invite all the residents[2] of the neighborhood to visit the building during the month of August. The office staff and many of the[3] teachers will be on hand to show you around the beautiful new facility between the hours of nine and five.[4]

We are particularly proud of the library. It is equipped with carpet, drapes, and comfortable furniture.[5] There are tables for group study, small carrels for individual study, and several rooms for conferences.[6] I know you will enjoy seeing the library as well as the rest of the building.

Make plans to visit your new[7] school in August. We look forward to seeing you. Sincerely yours,   [152]

LESSON 10

3 *Modern Education*

It has been said that the differences in people from various countries throughout the world[1] are not caused by climate, natural resources, or other physical factors. The differences are thought to be[2] caused by the type and quality of education provided to the residents of a particular[3] country. This is given as the reason why some countries progress while others do not.

In ancient times, some countries had[4] rather formal education systems. Others had little or no formal education programs. Many[5] older civilizations had a type of tutorial system in which promising students were taught[6] individually by recognized schol-

ars. Other countries had a type of apprenticeship system in which a young[7] person would work free of charge for a master at a craft in return for learning the details of a job. Both systems[8] worked fairly well, but the basic problem was that only a few students could be educated in these ways.[9] Education for the masses hardly existed.

Even in fairly modern times, education was considered[10] a luxury only for those who could afford the high costs. In the past century, a college degree[11] usually represented a rigorous mental exercise in theory. No courses of practical value[12] were offered. Instead, students concentrated on foreign languages, literature, and basic logic. While there[13] are practical values in each of these areas, of course, these aspects were not emphasized.

In more recent times,[14] the practical value of education has been recognized, and courses from business management to[15] automotive repair have made their way into the curriculum. When courses such as business management began to[16] appear in schools and colleges, many people felt that this type of education was of a low level.[17] Students who studied business or any other type of practical subject were sometimes scorned.

In more modern days,[18] people have come to realize the great value in practical education. While educators are certainly not[19] ready to give up the cultural courses of art, history, and literature, they have made room for courses[20] of immediate financial value to students. Courses in secretarial administration, management,[21] auditing, and other business fields are now ordinarily included in courses of study.[22]

Education is commonly recognized as a right of all citizens. It is not considered a privilege. In fact,[23] many countries have compulsory attendance laws that require all young people of a certain age to attend[24] school regularly. Most countries fund education through a system of local taxes. In some instances[25] education receives national assistance. The idea behind this is that the future of the city, state,[26] and nation depends on an educated populace.

Should a person go to college? This has been debated[27] for many years, and the answer really depends on the individual person. There are many jobs for which[28] college is an absolute necessity, but there are also many jobs for which college is not needed.

A[29] growing number of students are finding that the community college offers exactly what they need to[30] prepare themselves for their future work. In most of the technical fields, the community college offers a wide[31] variety of courses that are designed to help the student get that first job or advance to a better job.[32] Many students find that the community college gives an excellent foundation for senior college if they wish[33] to pursue higher education.

Today there are thousands of people returning to school after being[34] away from academic life for a period of many years. The field of continuing or adult[35] education is growing rapidly and has provided a valuable service to a great number of students.[36] Community colleges usually offer courses during the regular class hours as well as in the[37] evenings. The evening courses appeal to people who work full time and wish to continue their education[38] after working hours.

Many schools are now making courses available to students on an individual[39] basis. Teachers and administrators have worked diligently to prepare courses that students may take at times that[40] are convenient to them and at a pace that is exactly right for them.

In this type of program, the students do[41] not have to stay with a class that is progressing either too fast or too slow. Each student can determine his or[42] her own rate of progress. Not all students prefer to use this method, of course. However, those who do are able[43] to receive credit for courses planned and scheduled individually for them.

What is education[44] actually worth? That is a difficult question, and it can be answered only by the person involved. Modern[45] education offers a challenge and an opportunity to everyone.

How much education should one[46] have? This, too, is a difficult question to answer, and in the long run, it must be answered individually.[47] Many people contend that education lasts over a complete lifetime. Others feel that education[48] ceases with the end of formal schooling. It all depends on the point of view. The person who awakens every day[49] expecting to find something new and different that will enrich his or her life is a truly educated[50] person.

[1001]

CHAPTER 3

LESSON 11

4 Dear Mrs. Lexington: We realize that companies usually do not get letters from credit departments[1] unless their accounts are overdue. Such is not the case at this time. We are taking this opportunity to say[2] thank you for the fine way in which you handle your business.

Over the years it has been a pleasure for my company[3] to do business with the General Manufacturing Company. Your organization has taken care[4] of all its obligations in a very responsible manner. Only once were you ever as much as a[5] week late with a payment, and you acknowledged our first request for payment with a letter that satisfactorily[6] explained the delay.

It is customers like you, Mrs. Lexington, that make being a credit manager[7] a pleasure. If all companies took care of their credit obligations the way your company does, my job would[8] be an easy one indeed. Sincerely yours, [168]

5 Gentlemen: In a few months my organization, the Superior Publishing Company, will be opening[1] a sales office in Troy. We want to open a credit account with your furniture company.

The[2] Superior Publishing Company, which has been doing business successfully for many years, has established[3] a fine credit reputation with many businesses. The names of some of these companies are listed on the[4] enclosed sheet. If you should need credit references, please feel free to correspond directly with any of them.

Our[5] company is a large, progressive organization with offices in many major cities throughout the[6] nation. Our new Troy office will be just one of several that we will open during the coming year.

We have rented[7] a large office in Troy, and we are planning to redecorate it completely. We will need to buy a number of[8] executive desks and chairs. In addition, we will need a large conference table, several filing cabinets,[9] and various other furnishings.

If your company would like to help us in furnishing our new offices,[10] we hope you will let us hear from you immediately. Sincerely yours, [213]

6 Dear Dr. Greenburg: The Houston Credit Association will hold its annual conference next March, and we[1] would like you to chair the program committee. Would you be willing to accept this responsibility, Dr.[2] Greenburg?

The conference will be held at the Baker Hotel, which is located in uptown Houston. We expect[3] more than 500 people to attend.

We have discussed the program with several members of the executive[4] committee. They stated that they would like to hear an acknowledged expert in the field discuss government regulation[5] of credit. However, a program on any pertinent subject of general interest would be[6] appropriate.

If you will be able to handle this difficult •assignment, we will be very grateful. Please let[7] us know as soon as possible. Sincerely yours,   [149]

7 Dear Mr. Harrington: A good credit rating is a valuable thing. It is worth much more to you than most of[1] your other business assets. A good credit rating is not particularly difficult to obtain, but it[2] is very easy to lose.

Your account with the Cunningham Wholesale Company, which you have had for many years,[3] is now several months past due. We have written you many times, but you have not acknowledged any of our letters.[4] Under these circumstances, we are now faced with our last alternative. If we do not hear from you by return[5] mail, we must turn your account over to our lawyers for collection. This will, of course, endanger your credit[6] rating.

Immediate action on your part could prevent this from happening. Just write us a short note, tell us why[7] you have not paid your bill, and give us some idea of when we can expect a check. Do this today and protect your[8] valuable credit rating. Yours truly,   [167]

8 Ladies and Gentlemen: We are extremely happy to announce that we have been able *to* persuade Dr. E.[1] L. Bennington, who is pres-

ident of the Bennington Company in Providence, to serve as the main speaker[2] at the annual banquet of our association. As you know, Dr. Bennington is a highly respected[3] public speaker with an international reputation. He is recognized throughout the world as an[4] acknowledged authority in the field of credit. We are indeed fortunate that he could fit our program into[5] his busy schedule.

Dr. Bennington will present a speech on some new ideas in credit management. We[6] believe that this speech will have wide appeal. Even though his speech will be at the opening morning session, there should[7] be a very large audience.

Because we are expecting such a large turnout, we suggest that *you* make your[8] reservation immediately. Very truly yours, [170]

LESSON 12

5 Dear Mr. Glass: Ten years ago you opened an account with us. Since then you have been one of our best customers.[1] During the past few months, however, we have not heard from you. Our records show that you have not used your charge account[2] at the Hartford Department Store for the past three months, and we are quite concerned.

Perhaps we have done something to[3] offend you. We may have failed to do something that we should have done. Or it could be that you have not been able to come[4] to our store for some personal reason.

If we have offended you in some

way, we hope you will give us an[5] opportunity to rectify the situation. If we have failed to give you the service to which you are entitled,[6] we will take whatever steps are necessary to make you happy once again.

If you have not been able[7] to get to the store to do your shopping, we hope we can entice you to come in with one of our beautiful[8] new sales circulars. In the circular you will find some of the best buys we have ever offered, and they are[9] reserved for our special customers for the first six days of the sale.

Please come in soon. Sincerely yours,   [197]

6 Dear Miss Fleming: Enclosed is your new National credit card. Please take a minute or two now to sign it and place[1] it in your purse. Then each time you go shopping, be sure to take your National credit card along with you.

The[2] National credit card, which is accepted in stores in all 50 states, is one of the finest cards of its type[3] available today. Whether you are at home here in San Francisco or in another major city, you will[4] be recognized immediately as a person of responsibility and integrity when you[5] present your National credit card.

Please take a few minutes to read the credit agreement that is enclosed. It spells[6] out in detail your obligations as a National credit card holder. Note that 1 percent interest is charged[7] on the unpaid balance each month.

When you have finished reading the agreement, please file it in a safe place so that[8] you will be able to refer to it in the future.

Welcome to our large family of National credit[9] card holders, Miss Fleming. Yours truly,   [187]

7 Gentlemen: I have just accepted a new position with the Washington Manufacturing Company, and[1] I must do a great deal of traveling. I will be away from home 8, 10, or 12 days every month. Because I[2] do not like to carry a large amount of cash with me, I would like to apply for a National credit card.[3]

I understand that the National credit card is one of the best forms of identification available[4] and that it is accepted by more than 800 hotels, airlines, and service stations throughout the nation.[5] I also understand that there is no initial charge for this credit card and that it carries a line of credit[6] when registered with an approved bank.

Please send me an application blank and any information I need[7] to get a National credit card. Sincerely yours,   [150]

8 Dear Mr. O'Brien: Thank you for your letter asking for specific information about the National[1] credit card.

If your card is registered with an approved bank, you will have an automatic line of credit. If[2] your card is lost or stolen, you can get a replacement immediately at one of our 500 offices.[3]

We hope this information will be useful to you. Sincerely yours,
[73]

9 Dear James: I received your letter in the mail today. It was certainly nice to hear from you. I am glad to know[1] that you and and your family had a pleasant trip *to* your new home in Oregon. Oregon, which has some of the[2] most beautiful mountains in the world, has been one of my favorite states for a long time. I hope that I will be[3] able to visit you there sometime in the next year or two.

You may, of course, use my name as a reference to[4] establish credit in Oregon. I will write any letters of recommendation that you want. In addition,[5] I will be happy to give you a reference by telephone.

Please write often and let me know how you and your[6] family *are* enjoying your new home. Sincerely yours, [130]

LESSON 13

4 Dear Dr. Tate: There are three good reasons why more than 1,000 doctors in the state of Kentucky use the[1] Lexington Credit Service.

First, we can facilitate sending bills to all your patients. Second, we can take care of[2] all your accounting problems. Third, when patients are not able to pay their bills on time, we can help them obtain the[3] financing they need.

If you need this type of service, Dr. Tate, do not hesitate to get in touch with us[4] today. Our address is 1800 South Main, Houston, Texas 77704. We will be looking[5] forward to receiving your letter. Sincerely yours, [110]

5 Dear Mr. Kennedy: Since 1950 it has been a pleasure for our bank to serve the residents of[1] Newark. As you probably read in the newspaper yesterday, our bank has just joined seven other large banks in New[2] Jersey to form the largest, most experienced banking group in the area.

Exactly what does this mean to[3] you? It means that no matter what your company's financial needs may be, you will be able to satisfy them[4] right here at home. There is no need for you to go out of the city or out of the state to obtain adequate[5] financing. Whether you want to borrow a small amount of money against your accounts receivable or a[6] large sum to construct a new office building, we can help you.

There are over 2 million depositors in the[7] eight banks in our organization. This gives us financial backing equal to any bank in the nation. Yet[8] we intend to maintain our personal approach to banking. We will handle all your financial needs in the same personal,[9] attentive way that we always have. When you need our services, just call us at[10] 555-1871. Sincerely yours, [205]

6 Dear Ms. Cunningham: How often do you use credit? Is it 5 times, 10 times, or even 20 times in the course[1] of a day? If you are like most people, you are not certain exactly how many times you actually use your[2] credit.

You may have used your credit this morning by calling for a delivery of groceries before you[3] left for work. You may have used your credit after you arrived at work by placing an order for supplies to help[4] operate your business. If you intend to eat dinner at a restaurant this evening, you will probably use[5] a credit card to pay the check. The average person may use credit 1,000 or 2,000 times a year. As[6] you see, credit actually adds a lot to your personal and business life. It is worth a great deal to you.[7]

You have an opportunity now, Ms. Cunningham, to help maintain your good credit. As you know, you have owed our[8] company a small amount of money for four months. It is true that the amount you owe us is not very big,[9] but it does represent an obligation on your part.

Please write us a check for the enclosed bill and mail it to[10] us at our office at 4209 Main Street. It will help you maintain your good credit rating. Sincerely[11] yours, [221]

7 Dear Mrs. Edwards: It is exceedingly easy to obtain credit. All most people ordinarily need[1] to do is fill out a simple application blank and supply the names of two or three references.

It is[2] also easy to maintain a good credit rating. All most people usually need to do is to pay their bills promptly[3] each month.

In 1976 it was our privilege to extend credit to you, and since then you have always[4] paid your bills within one or two days after you received them. However, it has been four weeks since we mailed you our[5] latest bill, and you have not acknowledged re-

ceiving it. Perhaps you intended to pay it, but somehow it slipped[6] your mind. Perhaps you did not separate it from the other correspondence that arrived at the same time. Or[7] perhaps it was lost in the mail.

Whatever the reason is, please take a moment now to write us a check for the[8] enclosed bill, place it in the envelope that is also enclosed, and drop it in the mail. Do not hesitate, Mrs.[9] Edwards. Keep your good credit rating by sending your check now. Very sincerely yours, [195]

8 Dear Miss Young: Your letter asking for payment of my overdue bill arrived *in* the mail today. Frankly, it was[1] quite a surprise to me. I intended to pay the bill when it arrived four weeks ago. At that time I wrote the[2] check, inserted it into the envelope, and placed it in my desk. I was certain that I had mailed it the[3] following day. When I received your statement today, I looked in the desk drawer, and there was the envelope.

I am[4] enclosing check No. 1501 with this letter. Please forgive *me* for the delay. I want to retain my good[5] credit rating, and I assure you that I intend to take care of my financial obligations on a more[6] timely basis in the future. After I write a check, I will not hesitate a moment before placing it[7] in the mail. Sincerely yours, [145]

LESSON 14

4 Dear Mr. Torres: One of your

former employees, Mr. James Parker, has applied for a position with our[1] company, the Seattle Credit Corporation, and has given you as a character and business reference.[2] I hope you will take a few moments to fill out the enclosed form and return it to us.

We would like to know[3] specifically if Mr. Parker is a conscientious, efficient, and dependable person who can[4] handle his own work without direct supervision. In addition, we would like to know if he would be able[5] to work effectively with difficult credit customers.

Any information you wish to give us will be[6] appreciated, Mr. Torres. If we can ever extend a similar service to you, we will be more[7] than happy to do so. Thank you for your help; we appreciate it very much. Very truly yours, [158]

5 Dear Mr. Foreman: Miss Mary Moore, who formerly worked for your company, has applied for the position of[1] supervisor in our purchasing department. We are seriously considering hiring Miss Moore, but[2] before we do, we would like to have your frank opinion of her work. We need a person who has initiative and[3] who can accept responsibility.

Please fill out the enclosed personnel reference form; it will take only a[4] moment of your time. If you prefer to speak with me personally, please call 555-1798. I[5] look forward to hearing from you. Yours sincerely, [109]

6 Dear Mr. White: Your letter asking for a personal reference for Miss Mary Moore arrived today. Miss Moore worked[1] for me only a short time; she was a supervisor in our manufacturing department.

However, she[2] did not like the climate in this area; she wanted to relocate to a warmer state. She left after[3] only a few months to pursue a position in the purchasing department of a firm in Florida.

During[4] the time Miss Moore was with us, she seemed to be well liked by those who worked with her. However, I never had an[5] opportunity to observe her work directly. Perhaps you will be able to get a more complete reference from[6] her most recent employer. Yours very truly, [129]

7 Dear Mrs. Washington: For the past two years you have been a regular customer of our department store, and[1] we have appreciated your business very much. Our records show that you have purchased major appliances[2] from us on several occasions and that each time you have paid cash for them.

We were wondering, Mrs. Washington,[3] if you would like to open a charge account with our company. A charge account offers many conveniences.[4] First, you would not have to carry large sums of money with you when you wanted to make a purchase. Second, a charge[5] account would allow you to buy almost any large appliance whenever you wanted it; you would not have to wait[6] until you had ready cash. Third, one of our charge cards would serve as excellent identification whenever[7] you wanted to cash a check.

If you would like to have a charge account with us, just take a moment to fill out and[8] return to us the enclosed application form. We will be looking forward to doing further business with you;[9] we hope to hear from you soon. Sincerely yours,   [188]

8 Dear Miss Short: Thank you for your letter asking us to open a charge account for you with the Superior[1] Department Store. We are glad that you want to do business with our store, and we know that you will be satisfied with our[2] goods, our services, and our way of doing business.

Before we can open your account, however, we would like[3] you to fill out the enclosed credit application form and return it to us in the envelope that is also[4] enclosed. After we receive the application, we will make a routine credit check. If everything is[5] satisfactory, we will open an account for you and send you a credit card within a week or so.

We look[6] forward to doing business with you, Miss Short. Sincerely yours,   [131]

9 Dear Miss Carter: A charge account with the Jackson Department Store *is* a valuable asset. It helps you to have[1] the things you need when you want them. It keeps you from having to carry large amounts of money in your purse or[2] wallet. It identifies you as a dependable, responsible per-

son. In addition, it tells creditors[3] that you *are* a good credit risk.

Take the first step toward greater shopping convenience by applying for a Jackson[4] charge account. Just fill out, sign, and return the enclosed card to us in the envelope that is provided.[5] Please do it now. It will take you only a few minutes. Very truly yours,   [114]

LESSON 15

3 *The World Buys on Credit*

Have you ever thought just how much credit buying is used throughout the world? Every country[1] uses credit to some extent, and most countries use credit as a chief means of exchange.

On a national[2] level one country may use its good credit to buy food, machinery, or supplies from another country. The[3] amount of credit that a country may have depends largely on its resources and on its credit reputation.[4]

Many countries actually borrow money from their own citizens to finance various types of projects. A[5] country may borrow money to construct a building, to finance a federal program, or just to pay the[6] interest on other types of loans. When a country borrows money from its own citizens, it usually issues[7] bonds that pay interest to the purchasers. The interest is ordinarily exempt from local, state, or[8] federal income taxes, which makes purchasing bonds from the government a good investment in many cases.[9]

The federal government may also operate on credit. It may anticipate revenue from various[10] types of taxes that will be due within a short period of time. In a way, one might say that the government[11] is actually borrowing money against its own accounts receivable, which is a practice used by[12] many large business organizations.

On the state level much business is also conducted on credit. States[13] borrow money from their citizens by issuing bonds; however, a state may also borrow money from the[14] residents of another state by offering its bonds for sale on a national level. The interest rate that[15] a state must pay to those who buy bonds depends on the credit rating of the state itself. If a state is in good[16] financial condition and has a reputation for good fiscal management, the interest rate will probably[17] be low. If the state is not in good financial condition and, therefore, has a poor credit rating, it will[18] probably have to pay a high rate in order to attract buyers for its bonds.

Many states also have various[19] other sources of revenue. These include income taxes, sales taxes, and property taxes. From these[20] sources the states finance everything from education to sanitation. Many projects are financed on the[21] anticipated revenues from as yet uncollected taxes. Obviously, states use credit extensively.[22]

Cities also use credit in much the same manner that states do. In most cases, however, it is on a much[23] smaller scale. While a state may wish to finance construction of a large highway system, a city may wish to build[24] a new municipal building or a new school. The amount of money involved is much lower, of course.

The most[25] varied use of credit, however, is on the personal level. People borrow money for almost every[26] imaginable purpose and from a wide variety of sources. The first thing that comes to mind when one thinks[27] of buying on credit is the financing of a home. Many men and women throughout the world finance their homes[28] through mortgages. A mortgage is simply a legal obligation to repay a lending institution the[29] principal borrowed plus a set rate of interest. Few people have sufficient savings to purchase a home with [30] cash. Therefore, borrowing money to buy a home is a very common practice.

Many people also borrow[31] money to finance automobiles, television sets, and various home appliances. It has also become[32] a common practice for people to borrow money to finance the cost of education. In some cases[33] lending institutions give special terms to those who want to borrow money to attend a college, a technical[34] school, or some other type of educational institution.

Credit may be offered by banks and other[35] institutions that lend money directly to the public. Credit may be offered by department stores and other[36] business establishments that finance the purchase of items for each individual buyer. Credit may[37] also be extended on a continuous basis by stores that offer revolving charge accounts. Credit represents[38] a great convenience not only for the stores but also for the buying public. It helps people obtain[39] the things they need at the time they are needed.

It is easy to see that the world runs on credit. [797]

4 *Should You Borrow Money?*
Many people ask themselves nearly every day if they should borrow money. The answer is never easy, of[1] course. It depends on whether the money is genuinely needed for some worthy purpose or if it is to[2] be used for something that is not really necessary.

A person might wish to borrow money to attend college[3] in order to acquire a skill that would help in obtaining a new job. Few people would argue that borrowing[4] money for this purpose is unwise.

Another person might borrow money to attend college to learn a[5] hobby. Then the matter of whether the money is well spent comes into doubt. Some people feel that a hobby is[6] vital to mental and emotional health. Others feel that there is no justification for spending money[7] on a hobby.

Still another person might wish to borrow money to buy an expensive, luxurious item.[8] Most people feel that borrowing money for such a purpose is definitely not a good idea.

A person[9] who wants to borrow money should take into consideration the actual cost of money. When a bank,[10] a finance company, or some other lending institution makes a loan to a customer, it charges interest.[11] Borrowing even a small amount of money can be very expensive.

After careful consideration,[12] if you feel that what you want to buy is worth the cost, then it probably is wise to borrow. [257]

CHAPTER 4

LESSON 16

4 Dear Mr. Worth: Mr. Harry Smith, who formerly worked for your manufacturing company, has applied for[1] a position as correspondence clerk at our advertising agency. We are considering Mr. Smith[2] for a position of great responsibility, and we want your opinion of his character, his work, and[3] his attitude.

Will you please be good enough to answer several questions about Mr. Smith? Is he a person[4] of good character and judgment who can be trusted to handle highly confidential work? Is he a[5] dependable, responsible person who can organize his own work and complete it without direct supervision?[6] In your opinion, is he a person who could progress in a company such as ours if he should be given[7] the opportunity?

Will you please let us hear from you as soon as possible. We will appreciate any[8] information that you can give us. If we can ever be of similar service to you, I hope you will let[9] us know; we will be glad to reciprocate. Sincerely yours, [191]

5 Dear Mrs. Short: It is a pleasure to acknowledge your request for information about Mr. Harry Smith.[1] I am glad to write a letter recommending him for the position of correspondence clerk with your company.[2]

As you probably know, Mr. Smith worked for my company for ten years. During that time I found him to be[3] a person of excellent character, and he could be depended on to do his work without direct[4] supervision. I was satisfied with both the quality and quantity of his work, and he received several promotions[5] during his tenure with my organization.

He was usually at his desk a few minutes before the[6] start of the regular work day. He never objected to working overtime when the occasion demanded.[7] Mr. Smith is an excellent writer and administrator. Unfortunately, the opportunities for[8] advancement in a company such as this were very limited for a person of his talents. He discussed[9] this situation with me on several occasions, and when an opening occurred at a local newspaper,[10] I reluctantly agreed that it would probably be a good idea for him to take the job.

I know, Mrs.[11] Short, that if you hire Mr. Smith, he will be just the type of efficient employee you need. Will you please let me[12] know if you should hire him. Sincerely yours,   [247]

6 Dear Miss Price: In the next few months I plan to hire a number of people to staff our new regional office in[1] Los Angeles. If your organization can help us find the right people for the jobs we will have available,[2] we will be very grateful.

As you probably know, our company is a large, successful manufacturer[3] of office supplies. Our new regional sales office will serve the 12 states in this general area.

At[4] the present time we plan to hire 15 sales representatives, 5 sales supervisors, and 5 secretaries. We[5] will also have openings for creative people to write advertisements for the local newspapers and to[6] prepare circulars advertising our products. In addition, we will need maintenance and custodial[7] services. We hope that we can enter into an agreement with a local firm to supply these services on[8] an annual or semiannual basis for a set fee.

If you have any people to suggest for[9] any of the positions we will have open, please get in touch with Mr. William Bates, who will be the regional[10] manager of the new office. He will be opening a temporary office in Los Angeles the first[11] of November. You can reach him there by calling 555-9436 Monday through Friday. Sincerely yours,[12]   [240]

7 Dear Mr. Wilson: Your letter telling us that your manufacturing company plans to open a regional[1] sales office in Los Angeles arrived in the mail yesterday morning. Needless to say, *I* was very glad[2] to receive it.

My organization can handle all your personnel needs. We have on our present lists more than[3] 500 people who are qualified to fill one or more of the positions that you will have open in the[4] near future.

The people we recommend are not simply out of work. Our referrals are people who are successful[5] in their current jobs but who want to advance to positions of greater responsibility. On my staff[6] there are five specialists who can help you match the right person with the right job. I think you will find my staff to be[7] responsible, dependable people.

I am enclosing 50 forms for your use in writing exact job[8] specifications for each of the positions you will have open. The forms, of course, comply with all governmental[9] regulations. Will you please complete the forms and return them to us as soon as possible.

When Mr. Bates, your[10] new regional manager, opens his temporary office, we will be glad to assist him in any way[11] possible. We are looking forward *to* working with your organization. Sincerely yours, [237]

LESSON 17

5 Dear Mr. Davis: At this time every year our organization conducts a month-long drive to collect money[1] for the United Fund of Jackson. As you know, we have exceeded our goal for each of the past three years. This year,[2] however, it appears that we will not be able to meet our goal, which is only 5 percent more than last year's.[3] With only one week left, we have received pledges for only 60 percent of the goal.

We do not know the[4] exact reason, but we think that many people have simply forgotten to return their cards. If you have not yet[5] returned your pledge card, will you please do so in the next few days. Mr. Kenneth Washington is in charge of collecting[6] funds for your company; he will be happy to come to your office to pick up your card. If you prefer, you can[7] place it in the interoffice mail to him.

Your contribution to the United Fund of Jackson is[8] tax-deductible. It is a way by which you can contribute to more than 50 worthy charities at one time. You[9] can be sure that the money you give will be well spent and that every month each of the charities will receive full[10] benefit from your thoughtfulness. Cordially yours, [209]

6 Dear Dr. Cunningham: Several days ago Mr. Joseph Gold applied for a position in my electronics[1] manufacturing company. At that time he gave me your name and suggested that I call for[2] information about his work.

I understand that Mr. Gold was a student in three classes that you taught at Tate[3] College in New Orleans. I would like to know if Mr. Gold has potential for a management position. We are[4] looking for a highly capable person who can work with efficiency and dependability.

If you[5] think he can meet our requirements, we will probably offer him a position as a management trainee.[6] Any other information you can give us about Mr.

Gold will be sincerely appreci-ated.[7] Cordially yours,   [141]

7 Dear Mrs. White: A few days ago I saw your advertisement in the newspaper for a sales repre-sentative[1] for the states of Loui-siana, Mississippi, and Arkansas. The position sounds very inter-esting,[2] and if you have not yet filled it, I would like to be con-sidered an applicant.

I have had widely[3] diversified experience in the field of sales, and I am sure that you will find my background compatible with your[4] needs. I was born in New Orleans, and I know the sales ter-ritory there very well. I went to school in Mobile,[5] and for five years I worked as a sales repre-sentative for the Smith Com-pany in Alabama. I left that[6] position last year to continue graduate studies in marketing at Pace College.

My immediate[7] superior at the Smith Company was Mr. Max Lexington, who has agreed to write a letter of[8] recommenda-tion for me. My major professor was Dr. Ruth Evans; she has also offered to serve as a[9] reference for me.

The personal data sheet that is attached will give you additional information about[10] me. If you would like to have further infor-mation, please call me at 555-1401. Sincerely yours,[11]   [220]

8 Dear Mr. Lexington: Mr. James Jackson has applied for a position as a sales representative with[1] my company for the states of Louisiana, Mississippi, and Ar-kansas. He tells me that he was[2] employed by your company for a five-year period.

Will you please give me your opinion of his ability[3] as a sales-person, his personal initiative, and his character in general. We would also like to[4] know if you consider him to be well prepared for a sales position.

We are considering hiring Mr.[5] Jackson, but we would like to be sure that *he* is a competent, reliable person. If *you* will give us this[6] information, you will have our gratitude. Sincerely yours,   [131]

LESSON 18

4 Ladies and Gentlemen: At a recent meeting the management of the Smith Supply Company decided that[1] it would be to the company's benefit if all its em-ployees resided in the city of Springfield. As[2] you will recall, a representative of the mayor's of-fice asked that each of the major businesses located[3] inside the city limits establish such a rule for all employees. It was felt that this would encourage[4] housing construction within the city and bring added revenue to Spring-field, which has suffered some financial[5] adversity during the past decade.

The rule will be retroactive; it will include both current and future[6] employees. Each of the employees who currently lives outside the city limits will, of course, be given[7] adequate time to relocate inside the city limits.

If you wish to discuss this new

rule, please come to my[8] office.
James C. Smith   [163]

5 Mr. Smith: Your recent memorandum to the members of the staff of the Smith Supply Company has created[1] some animosity among the employees. About 50 percent of the company's employees[2] currently live outside the city limits. Of these, more than 80 percent own their homes. Some of them have been with the[3] company more than ten years. They feel that being forced to sell their homes and move at this time would be detrimental[4] to their welfare. Those who have families tell me that moving is definitely against their children's wishes.[5]

Looking at the problem from another perspective, you can easily see how difficult it would be to replace[6] about 50 percent of your employees should they decide to resign rather than move. Under the circumstances,[7] Mr. Smith, we are requesting that the board rescind its action immediately. The Employees'[8] Committee   [161]

6 Mr. Baker: Thank you for calling our attention to the problem you are having with the part-time personnel[1] in your department. We understand that some of your employees have become lax with regard to adhering to[2] our company's established working hours. We reported this problem to the company that supplies temporary[3] help to us. Unfortunately, they were not really concerned. They said that the problem was ours rather than theirs.[4]

In the past we have worked with several other companies' part-time employees, and we have not had such problems. We[5] have decided, therefore, to ask a new company to supply us with temporary help in the future.[6] Maria Lopez   [123]

7 Dear Mrs. Hastings: Our company's international division is planning to establish a sales office[1] in Spain shortly after the first of the year, and we are looking for a good person to manage the office. If[2] you know of anyone who might be a good candidate for this position, I hope you will let us know as soon[3] as possible.

The person we need must be able to speak Spanish fluently and have good management skills. We[4] will furnish free transportation to and from Spain on an annual basis, but we ask that the person be[5] willing to make at least a three-year commitment to the position.

If you can help us fill this position, Mrs.[6] Hastings, you will have our gratitude. Yours very truly,   [130]

8 Dear Mr. Tate: Welcome to the family of employees of our company; we are very glad to have you[1] on our staff. If you need any help in getting acquainted, just let us know. Very sincerely yours,   [38]

9 Dear Mr. Garcia: Welcome to the International Manufacturing Company. We are delighted[1] that you have decided *to* accept our company's offer to manage our new sales office in Spain.

As we agreed,[2] we will pay for all moving expenses for you and *your* family, and we will furnish a home for you in[3] Spain. You may move at any time during the three-month period beginning January 5.

After you[4] arrive in Spain, the responsibility of establishing the office will be yours. You will need to find a[5] suitable location for the office and hire an adequate number of people to staff it. We will, of course,[6] supply you with any help that you may need.

Please plan to spend a few days' time in our local office to familiarize[7] yourself with the operations here before you leave for Spain.

We are very happy, Mr. Garcia, to[8] have a person of your knowledge and experience to head our new office. Cordially yours, [177]

LESSON 19

4 Dear Mr. Strong: I read in yesterday's newspaper that your company is looking for three or four insurance[1] sales representatives to work in Milwaukee, Wisconsin. I would like to be considered an applicant for[2] one of the positions.

For the past ten years I have been living in Madison, Wisconsin, where I was engaged[3] in operating my own insurance company. However, I recently moved to Milwaukee, and I have[4] been looking for a good position with a well-known insurance agency.

I have had practical experience[5] selling medical and surgical insurance as well as life insurance. I have especially enjoyed[6] my work selling group insurance to large companies.

I know, Mr. Strong, that I could do a good job for your[7] company. Will you please give me an opportunity to prove what I can do for you? I am attaching a[8] personal data sheet that will give you a great deal of information about me. If you should need further[9] information, please call me at 555-1700. I will be looking forward to hearing from you. Sincerely[10] yours, [201]

5 Dear Mr. Troy: Thank you for your recent letter. I am happy that you have chosen our city in which to live,[1] and I am equally glad that you would like to work for our insurance organization.

As you probably[2] know, our company's policy is to employ people who have at least three years' experience in the field of[3] insurance sales, and you certainly meet that requirement. You may not know, however, that we hire people on a[4] trial basis for a six-month period before we actually make an initial long-term commitment[5] to them. Unless the representative proves to be successful, employment will cease at the end of the trial[6] period. In this way the representative may leave without any embarrassment. No contract is drawn up[7] until the end of the six-month period. At that time a long-term agreement, which is mutually[8] satisfactory, is made.

I am sending you separately a

booklet listing all our company's personnel[9] policies; an application blank is included in the back of the booklet. Please take a few minutes' time to read[10] each article carefully and then fill out and return the application form. When we have had an opportunity[11] to review your application, we will get in touch with you. Sincerely yours, [235]

6 Dear Mrs. Martin: In a few months' time I will be moving to Miami, Florida, for health reasons. For the[1] past several years I have lived in Bangor, Maine, but on my physician's advice I will establish my residence[2] in a city with a warmer climate.

I have worked as a medical secretary since my graduation[3] from Bennington College in Providence, Rhode Island, and it is essential that I find a similar position[4] in Miami. I hope your company will be able to help me find such a job.

My data sheet is[5] enclosed; I am sure you will find my education and work experience to be more than satisfactory. I[6] am also enclosing a list of four business and character references.

I will be here in Maine until the[7] first of January. I hope to hear from you soon. Sincerely yours, [153]

7 Dear Miss Lexington: Thank you very much for your invitation to speak at the special meeting of your[1] organization. I am very sorry that I must decline your invitation. I will be away from the city[2] until the end of the month.

I appreciate your thinking of me, however. Very truly yours, [58]

8 Dear Ms. Carson: If you are looking for a high-paying job but do not really know how to go about finding[1] one, our organization may have just the answer for you. The Executive Search Company *is* an[2] organization that specializes in placing business executives in just the right jobs.

We have found perfect[3] positions for more than 2,000 business executives here in Chicago, Illinois, since we opened our doors[4] ten years ago. We give the unsatisfied executive who is working in an unfulfilling, unrewarding[5] job the opportunity to move up to a position that will be both challenging and satisfying.[6]

If you would like to avail yourself *of* our services, just fill out and return the enclosed application card.[7] We will keep all records confidential, of course. Write to us soon. You will be glad you did. Sincerely yours, [158]

LESSON 20

3 *Personnel—A Valuable Asset*
An industry's most valuable asset is its personnel. The people who[1] work for an organization are much more important to that company's success than its equipment, supplies,[2] or machinery.

If an organization has intelligent, dependable personnel who are[3] dedicated to their work, the company will probably succeed. If an organization's employees are people[4] of good character and integrity, chances are that the company will have a good future. On the other[5] hand, if a company attracts and hires people who are not very interested in the operation of[6] the business, the company is likely to have a very difficult time.

Personnel includes, of course, all the[7] employees of an organization. It includes those persons who are in top management positions as well[8] as those who are involved in the actual production of the company's goods. All these people must work together[9] to make the organization successful and profitable. If each individual employee of[10] a company is not aware that he or she is a valuable, contributing member of the team, a[11] feeling of indifference can develop. This feeling will, of course, hinder the company.

Employees on every[12] level in a company should be consulted about things that will affect their daily work. Such little things as[13] a change in policy concerning coffee breaks can have a big effect on how a company's employees feel[14] about the organization.

The employees who work with machines should help in the process of selecting those[15] machines. If employees' offices are to be changed, each employee should be consulted about the change long[16] before it actually takes place. This will give each of them a feeling of being included rather than excluded.[17] It will foster a feeling of unity rather than one of division. If such little things are not done, the[18] staff may feel divided from management.

People who spend company money on a daily basis should assist[19] in planning short-term budgets. This will give them the feeling of actually being a part of the team, and it will[20] even help to ensure that company money is not wasted.

The management of a company must plan not[21] only for the company's immediate future but also for its long-range future. It must be sure that the[22] organization's objectives will be met for 5 years, 10 years, and even 20 years in the future. In this way[23] all the employees will have a feeling of security. Management should also make sure that each individual[24] employee feels included in both the short-range and long-range plans. If an organization makes a major[25] decision that affects most of its employees, each of those employees should accept that decision and understand[26] the reason behind it.

It is a company's employees who can cause the organization to prosper[27] or to fail. It is only with a feeling of teamwork that a business can move forward. A company's personnel[28] is definitely its most valuable asset. It is in the company's own self-interest to protect this[29] valuable asset.   [584]

4 *The Right Person*
Sometimes a company will spend a great deal of time trying to find a person to fill a[1] particular position. It is not unusual for a large company to take three, four, or five months to fill[2] an

important position.

Why would an organization take such a long time to fill a position? The answer[3] is that it is very expensive to hire and train the wrong person. If a company were to hire the first[4] person interviewed for a job, the company might find after six months or so that the new employee was not[5] really right for the particular position. All the funds that were expended to hire the person would be lost.[6] In addition, the time taken to train the employee would be lost. It is easy to see, therefore, that it is[7] very important to get the right person in the right job.

Just how can a company be sure that it is hiring[8] the right person? There is no magic way for any company to make sure that it is hiring the right person.[9] However, there are a number of things that can be done.

First, the person's references should be checked thoroughly.[10] If there is any doubt that the person is suited to the job, the company probably should interview[11] another candidate.

Second, the person should show a definite interest in the type of work that is to be[12] done.

Third, the personal traits that a person shows during the interview should be considered carefully. If the[13] job involves working with people, the candidate should have an outgoing, pleasant personality. If the job[14] is one in which the person must work alone, the company should look for someone who really likes this type of work.[15] A person who enjoys working with people all the time will probably grow tired of a job in which there is little[16] opportunity to work with others.

There is no definite way to be sure that the right person is hired[17] for a job. With a little care, however, a company can greatly improve its chances for success.

[358]

CHAPTER 5

LESSON 21

4 Dear Mr. King: On Tuesday, November 6, you will have the opportunity to help elect a new senator[1] from the state of New York. I hope that you will take a few minutes' time to look over the enclosed circular[2] that gives many facts about Ms. Mary Smith, who is running for this office this year.

As you will see, Ms. Smith worked[3] for a large newspaper in Albany for several years while she was completing her master's degree at Jennings[4] College. She then took a position of major responsibility with a publishing company in Troy,[5] where she worked for more than ten years.

At the present time Ms. Smith is vice president of one of the most widely[6] recognized children's magazines in the country. She has direct responsibility for the advertising,[7] manufacturing, and production departments of this firm. She has won the respect of all who work with her.

Ms. Smith's[8] experience makes her the best possible person for the job of senator. I hope you will take some time to[9] review all of Ms. Smith's qualifications and then vote for her on November 6; you will be glad you did.[10] Sincerely yours,   [203]

5 Dear Voter: It will soon be time to go to the polls once again. As you know, this year we will be electing a[1] senator from our state. The person that we choose will be serving a term of six years in Washington.

There are a[2] number of well-qualified people running for this office; however, in my opinion the best person for[3] the job is Mr. James Green of Troy. Mr. Green has held several important positions in the city, state, and[4] federal governments. He is now requesting that we give him our vote of confidence so that he will be[5] able to serve us as senator for the next six years.

Mr. Green has had many years' experience in private[6] business. When he finished college on June 1, 1965, he began working for the General Department[7] Store in Troy as an order clerk. He quickly advanced to a[8] position of greater responsibility in the correspondence department. After only a few years, he was promoted to the position of[9] manager of the accounting department.

Mr. Green then chose to leave private business and enter public life. He[10] was elected in rapid succession to government offices on the local, state, and national levels.[11] His performance in each of the positions was meritorious.

Mr. Green is not an ordinary[12]

person; he is definitely the best person we could send to Washington. Will you please vote for him in the November[13] 6 election. Sincerely yours,   [267]

6 Dear Member: At its next regular meeting on the 7th of September the Nashville Political Action[1] Club will have Mr. David Wellington as guest speaker. As you probably know, Mr. Wellington is the owner[2] of one of the nation's largest newspapers. At the meeting he will speak on the subject of developing[3] new ideas in state government.

Take advantage of this special opportunity to hear one of the most[4] dynamic public speakers in the world. Make your reservation now. All you need do is fill out and return the[5] enclosed card. When we receive it, we will send you your free tickets. Yours truly,
[113]

7 Dear Miss Harrington: Perhaps you read in yesterday morning's newspaper that I have withdrawn from the election[1] for a seat on the Denver, Colorado, City Council. I made this very difficult decision with a[2] great deal of reluctance. After careful consideration, I have decided that it will not be possible for[3] me to devote the amount of time necessary to represent the citizens of Denver in the way they[4] should be represented.

I have, therefore, withdrawn from the race, and I am giving my full support to Mr. Lee[5] Stevens, who is well qualified for this position. Mr. Stevens has worked hard over the past years to make[6] Denver a better city in which to live, and I am certain that he will continue to work hard.

I encourage[7] you, Miss Harrington, to vote for Mr. Stevens on June 5. He is a person of good character, high ideals,[8] and great ability. Sincerely yours,   [167]

8 Dear Mr. Gold: If you could do something to change the character of your neighborhood, would you do it? If you could[1] do something that would bring more business to your community, would you do it? If you could make your neighborhood a[2] better, safer place *in* which to live, would you do it?

Well, you will have the opportunity on November 5[3] to do all these things. On that date you can cast your ballot for William Huntington for City Council. Mr.[4] Huntington is a person of integrity, character, and dedication. He has been a successful business[5] executive in your city since January 23, and now he wants an opportunity to serve his[6] community as a member of the City Council.

Mr. Huntington *is* the best-qualified person for[7] the job. I hope you will vote for him; you will be glad you did. Sincerely yours,
[154]

LESSON 22

5 Dear Voter: On Thursday, September 3, the city of Midland, North Dakota, will hold an election to[1] determine if the people of the community are willing to pay for a new city hall at 121[2] Third Avenue.

As you know, the old city hall was built many years ago, and it is in very bad condition.[3] The cost of partially[5] renovating the old building would be very high, and the building would still be too[4] small to accommodate the necessary offices. Many of the officials would still have to use offices[5] located at various sites throughout the city.

In our opinion, renovating the old building would[6] be a waste of money. A group of concerned citizens of Midland is backing the bond issue, and we hope that[7] you will vote for it on September 3. If the construction is authorized, our city will have one of the most[8] modern, up-to-date city halls in the nation. Our money will be well spent; please vote for the bond issue. Sincerely[9] yours,   [181]

6 Dear Miss Morton: For the past two weeks I have watched with great concern the construction of a new apartment building[1] across the street from my home at 742 24th Street here in Madison, Oklahoma. I[2] understand that the local building code permits construction of buildings no more than ten floors in height in this area.[3] At this time I am sure the new apartment building now has steel framework for one or two extra floors.

Since you[4] are a member of the City Council, you have the responsibility of checking into such matters. Will[5] you please look into this problem yourself as soon as possible. The citizens of the neighborhood are concerned[6] that the addition of several extra floors to the building will intensify the traffic congestion we[7] already have because of the high density of population in the area. Very truly yours, [158]

7 Dear Mr. Smith: Several months ago I moved to Springfield. I live in a very nice neighborhood near the middle[1] of town. I have one very serious problem, however. Since you are a member of the City Council,[2] you should be able to help me with it. The drainage system in the area is not functioning properly.[3]

Will you please see if there is something that you can do to alleviate this problem. Cordially yours, [78]

8 Dear Mr. Brown: You are right; I can well understand your concern about the water that stands in front of your house[1] after a major rainstorm.

Unfortunately, this is a common problem throughout the city. As you may know,[2] the drainage pipes were installed in the city many years ago. At that time the city was very small. The[3] city has grown significantly, and additional home construction has caused the old drainage system *to* become[4] inadequate.

The drains operate as well as possible under the circumstances. I am afraid that in[5] order to improve the drainage, an entirely new system would have to *be* installed. This would mean that the city[6] would have to approve a bond issue to finance construction.

There are no plans to place

such an issue before the[7] public at the present time, but I will bring the matter to the attention of the City Council at its next[8] meeting. Very truly yours, [165]

LESSON 23

4 Dear Mr. Long: At the next meeting of the City Council a petition will be presented to incorporate[1] more than 100 acres of land into the city limits. The area in question is located[2] just outside the present city limits and runs along Smith Street.

Most of the property belongs to the National[3] Manufacturing Company, which ceased using it a long time ago. The management of the company[4] wants approval to divide the land into small lots and develop a new subdivision.

About 10 percent[5] of the land is owned by private citizens, and they do not want their property brought into the city. They feel[6] that the additional taxes they would have to pay in the city would be too high. These owners are now[7] each paying about $200 a year in taxes, but if their property were in the city limits, they would[8] have to pay about $300 a year.

Under the circumstances, I feel that a public hearing should[9] be scheduled as soon as possible. May I have your opinion about this matter. Yours truly, [197]

5 Dear Miss Jones: This is to acknowledge your letter of December 3 concerning the possibility that the[1] city of Long Branch, Nebraska, may annex an

additional 100 acres of land. I can, of course,[2] understand your feelings. After having lived outside the city limits for such a long period of time, you do[3] not wish to have your land annexed.

As you know, the National Manufacturing Company wishes to have their[4] property, which is located adjacent to yours, brought into the city limits in order to develop[5] a new subdivision. The value of such a development to the city would be more than $3 million[6] in additional tax revenues. If this request is approved, it could increase the value of your property[7] by as much as $5,000. You might wish to talk with the National Manufacturing Company[8] to see if they would like to purchase your land and include it in the proposed subdivision.

We have scheduled a[9] public hearing for Monday, January 4, at the city hall at 42 East 46 Street. All[10] interested parties can express their opinions on the matter at the hearing. You may be sure, Miss Jones, that the[11] city government will take no action until we have considered the matter thoroughly. Sincerely yours, [239]

6 Ladies and Gentlemen: Congratulations on the outstanding proposal you presented to the Long Branch[1] City Council last evening. You may be sure that you now have the backing of the majority of the members of[2] the Chamber of Commerce in your efforts to develop your property, which runs along Smith Street, into a new[3] subdivision. The new

housing is badly needed, and the plans you submitted are without doubt the most complete[4] ever presented to the City Council.

We have believed for a long time that the property should be developed,[5] and your new plans for a housing project are ideal. We are delighted that you have been given conditional[6] approval for the project pending final action by the City Council next month. If there is anything[7] we can do to help you, please let us know. Sincerely yours, [150]

7 Dear Mrs. Wilson: The Medford Chamber of Commerce is planning to open its annual membership drive on[1] Tuesday, February 4. The executive committee met last evening and voted unanimously to[2] ask you to head the membership drive this year. Because you have belonged to the Chamber of Commerce for the past ten[3] years, you are an ideal person for the position.

Our goals this year are to add 50 additional members[4] and to improve attendance at our monthly meetings. The addition of 50 new regular members should add[5] more than $2,000 annually to our treasury.

We realize, Mrs. Wilson, that you are a[6] very busy person and that you have many responsibilities. We hope, however, that you will accept this[7] very important position. We will be looking for a positive response from you soon. Cordially yours, [159]

8 Dear Mr. Link: Thank you *for* writing to me to express your

desire to have the park bill approved by the senate.[1] You are right; this is a worthy project. You may be sure that *I* will do everything in my power to get this[2] bill approved. You may not remember, Mr. Link, that I was one of the original supporters of the bill[3] that came before the senate two years ago. At that time the project was dropped because of a lack of funds.

If the[4] bill is approved and the parks are developed, the quality of life in our state will be greatly improved. I am[5] afraid, however, that your estimate of 25 cents a year for the average taxpayer is too low.[6] According to my figures it will cost each taxpayer at least 50 cents a year for a period of ten years[7] to pay for the project.

I suggest that you urge others who share your interest in the development of state[8] parks to write to their senators to express their wishes. Sincerely yours,

[173]

LESSON 24

4 Dear Mr. Carson: I read in yesterday morning's newspaper that the electric company is planning to[1] increase electricity rates almost 10 percent during the coming year. Frankly, Mr. Carson, I am[2] dismayed by this announcement.

You will remember that two years ago the electric company raised its rates almost[3] 5 percent, and only five years ago our electricity rates were raised 4 percent. Under the circumstances,[4] I do not believe another rate increase

is justified.

I hope you will look into this matter yourself,[5] Mr. Carson, and let me hear from you soon. Please call me at my office any weekday between the hours of 9[6] a.m. and 5 p.m. Sincerely yours, [127]

5 Dear Miss Harrington: Your disturbing letter reached my desk this morning. I can understand your concern about the[1] pending increase in electricity rates. A great many other residents of the city are distressed[2] about what appears to be an unjustified number of increases in the past few years.

The officers of the[3] electric company met with the elected officials of the city a number of times before the[4] rate increase was approved. Although I felt just as you do when I first heard about the increase, the management of[5] the firm convinced me that the rates must be adjusted. The electric company has been faced with greatly increased[6] fuel costs. Much of the increase is due to inflation. It is, therefore, essential for the company to raise its[7] rates if it is to remain in business.

None of us desires higher prices for any of the things we buy.[8] Unfortunately, inflation has taken its toll, and the rates must be increased. If you would like to discuss this with[9] me personally, please call me any morning after nine. Sincerely yours, [194]

6 Dear Ms. Stern: Last month I received a bill from the gas company that I feel is completely unjustified.[1] Compared with my bill for the corresponding month last year, this bill represents an increase of almost 25[2] percent.

I realize that the rates for natural gas have increased during the past year, but I do not feel that there can[3] be a logical reason for such a radical increase in my bill. Under the circumstances, I am[4] returning the bill to you so that you can make a special check of it yourself.

I am hopeful that you will be[5] able to get the bill reduced. When you have had an opportunity to check the bill, please call me at my office;[6] the telephone number is 555-1746. I am usually there from 9 o'clock in the[7] morning until 5 o'clock in the afternoon Monday through Friday. Yours truly, [151]

7 Dear Mr. Jones: As you are aware, the zoning commission of the city of Bayport, Oregon, has been[1] trying for a number of years to get the state government to designate Patterson Avenue, which runs along[2] the city limits, a state highway. Despite all our efforts, we have not been successful. We are trying once[3] again this year to obtain this designation, and we are hopeful that this time we will not be disappointed.

We[4] feel that the new designation would be helpful not only to the residents in the area but also[5] to the businesses in the vicinity. Another major reason for our attempt to get the designation[6] is to allow state highway funds to be used to widen the street and thus make it a major bypass around[7] the city. This would decrease the traffic congestion and pollution in the central business district.

I hope that[8] you in your position as a member of the advisory panel to the governor will do everything[9] in your power to help us obtain this designation. Sincerely yours, [193]

8 Dear Mr. Jones: Our organization was, of course, very much disappointed that you could not be helpful in[1] getting one of the streets in our city designated a state highway. We want you to know, however, that we[2] appreciate your taking the time to write to us about the matter.

We are planning to go ahead with our[3] attempts to obtain the designation, and we are hopeful that at sometime in the future we will be able[4] to obtain it. If we are successful, I am sure that you will be able to help us obtain financing to[5] widen the street and make it a major bypass for our city. Sincerely yours, [114]

9 Ladies and Gentlemen: I met recently with *the* district highway supervisor, Mr. James O'Brien. He[1] told me that your organization has finally been successful in obtaining the state highway designation[2] for Patterson Avenue. I want *to* congratulate you on your efforts of the past several years; they have[3] paid off well.

I will make a formal proposal to the finance committee at its next meeting at 10 a.m.[4] on Wednesday, February 4, to obtain financial backing for widening and rebuilding this street. Although[5] I cannot guarantee results, I hope that my recommendation will get a favorable response. Cordially[6] yours,   [121]

LESSON 25

3 *Government—How Big Is Big?*
How big must government be? This is a question that people in all states face daily.[1] The answer, of course, is never simple. When asked how big they want the government to be, most people will answer[2] that they want the government small enough to keep their taxes low. Hardly anyone would disagree with this[3] idea. When one begins to look at the services expected from government, however, the idea of just how[4] big the government should be often changes.

The government is responsible for making, interpreting, and[5] enforcing laws. In the United States these functions make up the three branches of the government, and each branch costs[6] money to operate. To make the laws, there must be a representative body to determine just what laws[7] are actually needed. To interpret the laws properly, there must be a court system. And, of course, there must be[8] various agencies to enforce the laws that have been made. Each time the government makes a law, it creates[9] the need for both interpretation and enforcement. All three areas must be well financed, and the finances[10] usually come from taxes.

The government also supplies any number of services to the people.[11] These services range from providing education to protecting health. Such a small thing as deciding that there[12] should be paved streets creates great expenses and actually increases the size of the government. Yet few people would[13] argue that paved streets are not needed in a city.

When a law is created to protect people's property from[14] theft or vandalism, an agency to enforce that law must also be created and financed. When laws are[15] written to ensure that people have freedom of speech, freedom of the press, and freedom to assemble, tax money must[16] be appropriated to ensure that these laws are enforced.

Some things that have formerly not been considered[17] government services are ordinarily expected today. These include such things as consumer-protection[18] agencies and environmental-control programs. Consumer-protection agencies are sometimes financed by[19] city governments and sometimes by state governments. They help to protect the buying public from fraud or[20] unscrupulous business operators. Environmental - protection agencies help to see that the interests of[21] the general public are maintained with regard to such things as pollution, traffic congestion, and manufacturing[22] in general.

Each of these things actually helps the public, but they all rely on tax dollars for[23] support. Every time an agency is created, government is expanded.

Just how much government should there be?[24] Every city,

state, and nation must decide for itself the answer, which is never simple. It depends on just how[25] many services the citizens expect from the government and how much they are willing to pay for them. [519]

4 *The Branches of Government*
In the United States there are three branches of the federal government. Each of[1] the three branches has specific duties and responsibilities. Each serves as a check over the other two.[2] In this way no one section of the government has complete power.

The three branches of the government are the[3] legislative branch, the executive branch, and the judicial branch.

The legislative branch is charged with the[4] responsibility of making the laws. It is composed of the Senate and the House of Representatives. There[5] are two senators from each state. The number of state representatives is based on the total population[6] of the congressional districts.

The executive branch is responsible for enforcing the laws. It is composed[7] of the President and the various law enforcement agencies throughout the country.

The judicial branch[8] must interpret the laws. This branch is made up of the various courts. The highest court is the Supreme Court in[9] Washington.

Each of the three branches works to ensure the successful, efficient operation of the national[10] government. [202]

CHAPTER 6

LESSON 26

4 Dear Mr. Jones: If you are looking for a safe, convenient place to keep your money, stop in at the new branch of[1] the General National Bank. As you probably know, last January we opened this beautiful new branch[2] on the corner of White Street and Spring Drive. The building, which was designed with our customers' best interests in mind,[3] now serves depositors throughout the Middle Village area.

We are happy to report that in a six-month[4] period, we have attracted more than 25,000 new depositors; our assets are now in excess[5] of $2 million. We are very proud of our success, and we are working hard to satisfy the needs of[6] the new depositors we have won. We offer regular checking accounts, savings accounts, and both short-term and[7] long-term loans.

The next time you are in the area, drop in and learn exactly what we have to offer; we will[8] be very glad to see you. Sincerely yours, [168]

5 Dear Miss Patterson: When you have a savings account at the First State Bank, you have a very valuable thing. In[1] addition to having a substantial sum of money for emergencies, you have an established credit[2] rating. The First State Bank offers regular savings accounts that bear interest at the rate of 5 percent. We[3] also offer 12-month savings accounts that yield substantially higher rates of interest.

Why not drop by our[4] office at 200 State Street and talk with one of the friendly executives in our savings department. Opening[5] a savings account with our bank could be the best investment you will ever make. Sincerely yours, [118]

6 Dear Miss Hastings: Recently I had a conversation with Mr. James Smith, one of the executives in our[1] credit department at the Central State Bank. He told me that you have been one of the best customers we have had[2] over the past ten years. We want you to know, Miss Hastings, that we appreciate your business and the prompt, efficient[3] way you repay your loans.

It occurred to us that you might wish to have an open line of credit with the bank.[4] If you wish, we can arrange to have loans extended automatically whenever you write a check for more[5] than the amount in your regular account. We can establish a line of credit for you for $1,000,[6] $2,000, or even $3,000. Just let us know if you would like to have this service; we[7] hope to hear from you soon. Sincerely yours, [147]

7 Dear Miss Lopez: In today's mail we received your application for a Washington National Bank credit card.[1] As you probably know, a credit card from Washington National Bank is one of the best credit devices[2] you can have; it is accepted in more than 5,000 business establishments throughout the Washington area.[3] In addition, you may cash checks at cooperating out-of-town banks up to a maximum of[4] $100 if you should need cash when you are out of this city.

We are now processing your application,[5] but we find that we need some additional routine credit information. Will you please fill out the enclosed[6] form and list three or four credit references. When we hear from you, we will finish our work and get in touch with you.[7] Yours very truly, [144]

8 Dear Mr. Chang: Enclosed are the completed forms you asked me to fill out with regard to my application for[1] a Washington National Bank credit card. I am happy to list three credit references; they are shown on the[2] back of the form.

In the past I have used the Commercial State Bank for all my regular checking needs; however,[3] this bank does not offer credit card services. Therefore, I am considering moving all my banking business[4] to the Washington National Bank.

I am sure that you will find my current bank account with the Commercial State[5] Bank in very good order if you call the bookkeeping department there. If there is any other information[6] you would like to have, please let me know. Sincerely yours, [130]

9 Dear Mr. Wellington: On Wednesday, November 21, I was in the Kansas City branch of the State[1] National Bank. I made a deposit of $500, but through a clerical error I failed to receive[2] a duplicate deposit slip.

Will you please check on this and send me a verification of this deposit as[3] soon as possible. I want to be sure that the correct amount has been credited to my account.

Thank you,[4] Mr. Wellington, for taking care of this matter for me. Sincerely yours, [93]

10 Dear Mr. White: Thank you for writing to me about the failure of one of our employees to give you a[1] duplicate of the deposit slip verifying the deposit you made in our Kansas City branch on Wednesday,[2] November 21.

I have checked into the matter myself, and I am enclosing a copy of the[3] deposit slip. You may be sure that the deposit was properly credited to your account. When you receive your[4] next bank statement, the deposit will be included.

We want you to know, Mr. White, that we appreciate your[5] business. Whenever we can serve you in any way in the future, just let us know. Sincerely yours, [118]

11 Dear Miss Lopez: Enclosed is your new Washington National Bank credit card. We are happy to tell you *that* your[1] new account is open and ready for your use. We have checked your credit references, and those with whom we talked had a[2] very good opinion of your bill-paying habits. They told us that *you* are a responsible business[3] executive of good character who takes care of all finan-

cial obligations quickly and satisfactorily.[4]

Enclosed is a copy of the credit agreement that you signed; please place it in your files for future reference. If[5] you should ever wish to have any additional information about your Washington credit card, just[6] contact any of the people in our correspondence department by calling (275) 555-1472.[7]

Welcome, Miss Lopez, to the large family of Washington National Bank credit card users.[8] Sincerely yours, [162]

LESSON 27

5 Dear Mr. James: Thank you for your letter asking for information about opening an account with the[1] Missouri National Bank. I am happy to answer your questions. Even though our bank is one of the largest in[2] the state, we have a warm, friendly atmosphere, and we give each depositor personal attention.

Opening[3] an account with our bank is one of the easiest things you will ever do. Because we have a number of[4] branches located throughout St. Louis, you will probably not have to travel more than two or three miles. When you[5] arrive at the nearest branch, all you need to do is fill out a simple application blank, sign it, and give it,[6] along with your deposit, to one of the people in our accounting department. You will not have to go through a[7] long application process. After only a few minutes' time, you will receive a temporary checkbook,[8] which you may use until your regular supply of checks arrives in the mail.

I am sure you will agree that[9] opening a checking account with the Missouri National Bank is quite easy. May we have the opportunity[10] of opening an account for you soon? Sincerely yours, [211]

6 Dear Mrs. Murphy: A few months ago I received my regular bank statement from the American Bank here[1] in Honolulu.While I was looking through it, I found a small error in the final balance. I notified[2] one of the people in your accounting department as soon as I noticed the error, and I was told the[3] problem would be taken care of immediately.

I thought the matter was settled. But two months ago I received[4] another statement, and the error had not been corrected. Again I called the accounting department.[5] Unfortunately, I did not remember the name of the first person who helped me, but the second person was a nice[6] chap by the name of James Moore, who told me the problem would be taken care of as soon as possible.

In today's[7] mail I received this month's statement, and for the third time the error is still there. I am perplexed by the situation.[8] Though the error is small, I cannot understand why a large organization like the American Bank[9] cannot take care of it properly. Will you look into the matter yourself, Mrs. Murphy, and let me hear from[10] you as soon as

possible. Sincerely yours, [208]

7 Dear Miss Fox: Thank you for calling to my attention the problems you have been having getting the error[1] corrected on your statements from the American Bank. I can easily understand why you are perplexed by the[2] situation.

I could tell you that the trouble was caused through an error in the computer, which is true. However,[3] that would not explain why we have not been able to correct it. I could tell you that in the rush of the busy[4] holiday season we simply did not have time to make the correction, but that would be a poor excuse.

What I[5] will tell you, though, is that I have taken care of the trouble myself and that you will have no further problem. Please[6] forgive us, Miss Fox, for this blunder; we guarantee that such a thing will not happen again. Sincerely yours, [139]

8 Gentlemen: Recently, I was on a cross-country automobile trip from Juneau, Alaska, to Seattle,[1] Washington. While I was driving through Alaska, I was involved in an automobile accident. I had to[2] stay a few days to get my car repaired. Although I thought I had enough cash for any eventuality,[3] I soon realized that my supply of cash was not sufficient.

Frankly, I was afraid that I would have a difficult[4] time trying to cash a check written on a bank in Washington. However, when I presented my American[5] Bank identification card, the clerk simply placed it in a computer terminal and quickly[6] verified my account.

I wanted to tell you that I consider the computer services that your bank uses[7] to be one of the best innovations in the field of banking. Sincerely yours,   [154]

9 Dear Mr. Wellington: Thank you very *much* for sending me a copy of my latest deposit slip. Thank you[1] also for taking care of this matter yourself. Although the amount of the deposit was not very big, I[2] wanted to be sure that no error had been made.

You may be sure, Mr. Wellington, that I appreciate the[3] friendly, personal way in *which* business is transacted at your bank and that I will continue to use your[4] services for many years to come. Very truly yours,   [90]

LESSON 28

4 Dear Mr. King: For the past few months I have been considering buying a new house, and I would like to inquire[1] about the possibility of your financing the purchase. I rented an apartment for many years, but[2] now I would like to have a much larger place in which to live. I have selected a house in the Green Gardens[3] subdivision; however, it is very old and needs to be painted. In addition, the plumbing and wiring need[4] to be checked thoroughly.

Will you please tell me if your bank would be interested in handling the financing,[5] Mr. King. If it is possible, I would appreciate your taking care of this matter yourself. Very sincerely[6] yours,   [121]

5 Dear Mrs. Sweet: Several weeks ago I was traveling to work and I spotted a beautiful new house under[1] construction on South Park Avenue near Madison. The house is situated on a large plot, and the grass and[2] shrubs have already been planted. A sign in front of the house states that it is for sale and that your agency is[3] the real estate broker.

I am interested in purchasing a new home, and I would like to know the price of[4] the house, the amount of the taxes, and any other information you can give me about the property.[5]

May I hear from you as soon as possible. You may write to me at the address shown on this letter, or you may[6] call me between the hours of 9 a.m. and 5 p.m. at 555-9408. Sincerely yours,   [138]

6 Dear Ms. Lexington: Thank you for all your help in getting quick approval of the loan to finance the purchase of[1] my new house. As you will remember, I had some trouble getting clear title to the property.

The former[2] owner, Mr. James Strong, had not officially registered the sale of the property. Mr. Strong's failing to do[3] so caused a three-month delay in my finalizing the purchase. With your aid, however, I was at last able[4] to obtain clear title to the property.

Thank you, Ms. Lexington, for helping me in this way. I realize that[5] it was not actually a part of your responsibility in this matter and that you spent many hours of[6] your own time working on it.

You may be sure that I will remember the fine treatment I received at your bank and[7] that I will recommend your bank whenever the occasion arises. Sincerely yours, [156]

7 Dear Mr. Drake: Last week I paid my regular visit to your bank at 1200 West 23 Street in[1] Macon, Georgia. I always bring my paycheck to the bank personally because I feel there is some danger in[2] entrusting it to the mails.

On my arrival at the bank I went to the window where I ordinarily do[3] business. Miss Jane Smith, the regular clerk, was not there. I deposited my paycheck with the temporary clerk,[4] but I was not allowed to cash a small check that had been given to me as a gift from a friend. The clerk told me[5] that I could deposit the check and write another for the exact amount on my own account.

I realize that[6] a bank must have certain rules and regulations and that temporary employees usually follow these rules[7] and regulations to the letter. However, I have been a regular depositor at the First National[8] Bank for six years, and I do not appreciate the kind of treatment I received. I hope you will make every[9] effort to keep this kind of thing from happening in the future. Sincerely yours, [194]

8 Dear Mr. Cunningham: Thank you for your letter telling me of your experience at the First National Bank[1] last week. I am very sorry *that* you did not receive

first-class treatment at our bank. We realize that you have been[2] one of our very best customers for many years, and we want to do everything in our power to make your[3] regular visits to our bank pleasant in every way.

We do not ordinarily cash checks drawn on out-of-town[4] banks. We ask that they be deposited and collected before we credit an account. If Miss Smith had been[5] there, I am sure she would have cashed the check for you. The temporary clerk, Mr. Lee Macy, did precisely what[6] his job description called for him to do. However, job descriptions do *not* take into account personal and[7] business friendships. We apologize for Mr. Macy's not taking time to check this matter, and we hope you will[8] forgive us.

If you should have any trouble of any kind with the service at our bank, just ask to see the manager;[9] the trouble will disappear in no time at all. Yours truly, [192]

LESSON 29

4 Dear Miss O'Brien: Thank you for your letter of application for employment at the Import and Export Bank.[1] I was quite impressed with your qualifications and with your experience. Unfortunately, it is impossible for us to offer you a position at this time. We do not[2] currently have a position for a person with your general background.

With your permission, however, I am[3] sending your letter and personal data sheet to Mr. A. L. Martin, manager of our personnel[4] department. When there is a position available for a person with your qualifications, I am sure[5] Mr. Martin will get in touch with you.

Thank you, Miss O'Brien, for considering the Import and Export Bank as[6] a possible employer. Sincerely yours, [128]

5 Dear Mr. Goldberg: The members of the board of directors here at the Empire State Bank have decided that our[1] present building is much too small. At its last meeting the board voted to go ahead immediately with plans[2] to find another location that would be suitable for a new bank building.

We are currently looking at[3] one site in the uptown area and another near the Garden Shopping Mall. The uptown site is only a[4] few blocks away from our present building, and we could make the transfer to that location with little inconvenience.[5] However, we feel the price of the land is somewhat high.

The suburban site, which is more than 15 miles[6] away, is more reasonably priced, but we are concerned about the impact of our moving away from the central[7] business district.

We would like your company to make a public opinion survey, Mr. Goldberg. We want to[8] know exactly what the impact of such a move would be. We want to know if the public will accept the move or[9] if they would feel that the move was improper. We would also like to know what effect such a move would have on our[10] own employees' efficiency and morale.

If you would like to take this survey for us, I hope you will get in[11] touch with us as soon as possible. Sincerely yours, [230]

6 Dear Mr. Mason: After making a comprehensive survey of the impact of moving your main banking[1] facilities to the suburbs, I can tell you with confidence that the move could have a devastating effect on[2] your business.

Many of your depositors think the move would be improper, and most of your employees are[3] also against it. They feel there is no justification for your moving to the suburbs. In addition, the[4] merchants in the uptown area feel that the move would have a terrible effect on their businesses. They feel that[5] your moving to the suburbs would be inconsistent with your policy of dedication to the community[6] that you serve.

At this point I would suggest that you look into the possibility of expanding your[7] present building. I have taken a few moments to look over the specifications and find that you could add at[8] least five floors without causing any structural damage to the foundation. You could also make a number of[9] major modifications inside the bank and perhaps add a new facade.

I suggest that you investigate[10] all the various alternatives available to you at your present site before seriously[11] considering moving to the suburbs. Yours truly, [228]

7 Dear Miss Lopez: At its latest meeting the board of the Empire Bank voted to expand our main building by more[1] than 100,000 square feet. Although our plans are incomplete at the present time, we are tentatively[2] planning to add three or four new floors and remodel the interior of the present building.

Our current[3] facilities are much too small, and it is impossible for us to provide the type of service our depositors[4] desire. Our current methods are inefficient and outmoded. In addition, our facilities are inconvenient[5] for our depositors.

When we have finished our remodeling program, we will offer the most convenient,[6] up-to-date services available anywhere in the state. We will keep you posted from time to time on[7] the progress of our work. Sincerely yours, [147]

8 Dear Mr. White: On Monday, August 13, the newest, most convenient branch of the Huntington Savings Bank will[1] open in your neighborhood. I am sure you will be glad to know that *you* can use all the facilities of this[2] branch, which is located only a few blocks from your home, without changing your present account with the central branch[3] of the bank.

Because our modern computer facilities at the new branch are connected to the bank, it will[4] be possible for you to transact all your business at the branch in your neighborhood. All you need do *is* stop by[5] the new branch and pick up a special identification card from any of the employees there. Then you will[6] be able to make transactions at your neighborhood branch or at the main bank.

If you have any questions, just call[7] us; we will be glad to answer them. Sincerely yours, [150]

LESSON 30

3 *The Changing Banking Industry*

Every day millions of people use the services of banks throughout the nation.[1] It is true, of course, that a great deal of business is conducted on a cash basis, but the vast majority[2] of business transactions are handled by check.

Why is so much business done by check? The answer is easy. Checks are[3] a safe, convenient way of paying for items. It is not necessary for a person to carry large sums[4] of cash. With proper identification, almost anyone can pay for purchases by check.

The widespread use[5] of checks has caused a significant increase in the amount of paper used in banks throughout the United States.[6] For many years banks simply added more and more employees to their staffs in order to keep up with the[7] ever-increasing paperwork. Eventually, it became obvious[8] that banks simply could not process all the paperwork manually. By January 1, 1955, a number of banks had initiated[9] programs whereby unit-records equipment handled a large percentage of the work. By 1960 many[10] of the banks were actually using computers to do much of the work.

However, the number of checks[11] continued to grow, and the banks had to add larger, more efficient computers just to keep up. The introduction[12] of the computer in business created many new and interesting jobs that had not been available[13] before. Both public and private schools began to train unit-records equipment operators and keypunch[14] operators. For a few years there was a great shortage of people who could work with computers and computer-related[15] equipment. Although the demand has now lessened, the computer field still offers many opportunities[16] for those who are interested in this field of work.

Even with the advent of the computer, the paperwork[17] in banks continued to grow. In most cases the exact banking procedures that had formerly been handled[18] manually were now being handled by electronic computers. Bankers again became aware that[19] something must be done to alleviate the tremendous burden of this great amount of work.

At first, a few banks[20] experimented with the idea of automatically transferring funds from one account to another. They[21] would, with permission from both parties concerned, transfer on a regular date each month a set amount from one[22] account to the other. This could easily be done for mortgage payments or car payments. Instead of a person's[23] writing a check and mailing it to the creditor, the bank would simply transfer the funds and notify both parties.[24] This reduced the number of checks written, but it created a few other problems. Both parties had to remember[25] to deduct or add the proper amount on their records. In addition, the bank sent notification to[26] both parties, which created two more pieces of paperwork. Many banks have now stopped sending notification;[27] they simply guarantee that funds are transferred on the proper day. In this way some of the paperwork is[28] eliminated.

One of the major uses in the larger cities such as Chicago, Illinois, and Los Angeles,[29] California, is the automatic transfer of funds to complete a company's payroll procedure. This[30] requires that a bank and its employees agree that on a set day each week or each month the bank will credit each[31] employee's individual account with the exact amount of his or her pay and charge the company's[32] account for the total amount. The company notifies all employees of the amount credited to their[33] accounts, which relieves the bank of this responsibility. The company no longer has to write checks, which is a[34] great boon to its accounting department.

Although automatic transfer of funds is gaining in popularity,[35] there are still many banks that do not like the idea in general and have not yet initiated[36] any programs of this type. In addition, a large number of depositors continue to prefer to handle[37] their banking in the usual way.

The field of banking in the United States has undergone great changes in[38] the past few decades, and many more changes are predicted for the future. [774]

CHAPTER 7

LESSON 31

4 Dear Mrs. Short: We are very glad to announce that on Monday, January 4, our office building, which is[1] located at 210 Worth Street in Charlotte, North Carolina, will officially turn on its unique solar[2] heating system. We are particularly proud of this system because it is one of the most up-to-date[3] solar heating systems available today.

At the present time there is no other building in the East that has[4] such a modern, efficient heating system. The system will save our company thousands of dollars every year[5] in heating bills, and we will pass these savings along to our customers. In addition, the new system will help[6] to conserve our country's energy.

I hope, Mrs. Short, that you will join us on January 4 to help us[7] celebrate the installation of this unique heating system. Yours truly, [154]

5 Dear Mr. Wilson: For the past seven years I have lived in the south part of Wheeling, West Virginia, and have been[1] a customer of the Wheeling Electric Company. Five years ago my electric bill was about $15[2] per month; four years ago it was $20 per month. It remained at that level until last year.[3] However, for each of the past three months my bill has risen 5 percent.

I can see no justification for such[4] a drastic increase in my electric bill. Will you please look into this matter yourself, Mr. Wilson, and let[5] me know what the trouble could be. Sincerely yours, [109]

6 Dear Miss Bennington: Several weeks ago I was driving west on Jackson Street, and I noticed about 300[1] feet of electric wire lying along the north side of the street. It did not appear to be attached to any[2] electric power source, and I assumed that the wire would be used to replace defective wiring.

Yesterday[3] morning I was again in the same vicinity, and I noticed that the wire was still lying beside the street. There[4] is no evidence that it is going to be used at any time in the near future.

I consider wiring[5] of this type a danger to the children in the area, and I hope you will take action to remove it as[6] soon as possible. Will you please let me know what disposition you make of this matter. Yours truly, [138]

7 Dear Mr. Torres: I do not usually write letters of this type; however, I feel compelled to write this one.[1] For over a year the street in front of my home at 412 South Park Drive has been under repair. There is a trench[2] about six feet wide that runs down the entire length of three city blocks.

As you can easily understand, this trench[3] disrupts the normal traffic flow and is actually a hazard to all children in the area.

Occasionally,[4] I see two or three people working in the area, but no one is there most of the time. I have[5] questioned these people about what could be causing the delay in repairing the street, but I have not received a[6] satisfactory answer.

The residents of the area have decided that if the repairs are not finished[7] within a one-month period, we will take legal action against the city. Will you please let me know[8] immediately what action you plan to take. Yours truly, [170]

8 Dear Mr. Moore: Thank you for writing to me about the condition of South Park Drive.

We entered into a binding[1] contract with the General Pavement Company of Columbia, South Carolina, and they were to have[2] finished the work within three months' time. When the work was partially finished, we made a partial payment. However,[3] the company filed for bankruptcy shortly after that time, and we have had no success in getting them to finish[4] the work.

The City Council has decided to finish the work on the street immediately rather than[5] wait any longer. In a few days there will be another company under contract to complete the repairs.[6] Yours truly, [122]

9 Ladies and Gentlemen: I would like to *inquire**about possible employment with the South Carolina Power[1] Commission. I will soon be graduated from Clark Business School in Los Angeles, California, and I[2] would like very much to work for your *organization.*†

I am enclosing a copy of my transcript of credits[3] from Clark Business School. As you will see, I completed courses in stenography, typing, and business correspondence.[4] In addition, I took several courses in business management. I am also enclosing a list[5] of character, business, and personal references.

I have had three years' experience working full time, and[6] I am presently a part-time employee of the Los Angeles Power Commission, where I have learned a great[7] deal about the subject of energy. I hope to hear from you soon. Sincerely yours, [155]

Also correct:
*ask
†company, firm

LESSON 32

5 Dear Mr. King: Several days ago we sent you a notice that your payment for gas and electricity for[1] the months of October and November was six weeks overdue. However, we have not yet had an acknowledgment[2] from you.

We realize, of course, that there could be many good reasons why you have not yet paid your bill, and we are[3] sure you have an explanation. We will understand if you give us a chance. However, you have not given us[4] an opportunity, and we are now faced with the prospect of having to turn your account over to one of[5] our attorneys. If we have to do this, your credit rating will suffer.

Each day that passes places your good[6] credit rating in further jeopardy. Please inform us as soon as possible when we may expect payment from you.[7] If you cannot make a full payment at this time, at least send a partial payment. We will expect a letter by[8] return mail. Yours truly, [164]

6 Dear Mr. Mills: Several days ago I heard that your company may build a new natural gas pipeline between[1] Dallas, Texas, and Detroit, Michigan. If this is true, our organization, the General Construction Company[2] of Detroit, would like to make a bid on some of the construction work.

Will you please let us know the current[3] status of the plans for this pipeline. We know that you will want to give each of the independent companies in the[4] area an equal opportunity to make bids on the various parts of this major project.

I hope[5] to hear from you by return mail. Very truly yours, [110]

7 Dear Miss Blank: In today's mail we received your letter telling us that you will be moving to our city from[1] Reno, Nevada. We are happy to welcome you as a new resident of Montpelier. We are now processing[2] your order for gas, water, and electricity for your new home at 800 West 14

Street.

We are[3] enclosing a short credit form that you should fill out and return to us as soon as possible. It will take only[4] a few minutes' time to complete. In addition, please attach a check for $50 as a deposit for[5] this service. This money will be put in a special account, of course, and applied to your account only if you[6] should ever be late paying a bill. The deposit will be returned to you in full after you have lived here for[7] one year.

You will be billed once a month for all utility service; the bill is payable within ten days[8] after you receive it.

We are very happy, Miss Blank, that you have chosen Vermont as your new home. Please contact us[9] a few days before you arrive, and we will make sure that the utilities are connected. Sincerely yours, [199]

8 Dear Mr. Lexington: In December we wrote you asking for payment of your electric bill, which was one month[1] overdue at that time. In January we billed you again, and in February we billed you a third time.[2] However, you have not acknowledged any of our letters. We have even tried to contact you by telephone[3] several times, but we have not been able to get in touch with you.

You realize, of course, that we cannot continue[4] to supply you with electric service if you do not pay your bills. If we do not hear from you by March 1, we[5] will have to turn your account over to a collection agency. Please let us hear from you immediately.[6] We do not wish to deprive you of electric service, and we do not want to take legal action against you.[7]

We will be expecting a letter from you by return mail. Yours truly, [153]

9 Dear Miss Link: If you are like most other people who live and work in the heart of the city, you probably want[1] to get away from the hurry and fast pace of city life as quickly as possible on the weekend.

Just two[2] years ago the Reliable Real Estate Company opened the first section of its vacation condominium[3] community in West County. Since that time more than 500 city dwellers have purchased vacation[4] homes there.

Now we are pleased to make the announcement that the second section is open. Why not take an hour's trip to[5] West County this weekend and see what a wonderful vacation home you can buy at a surprisingly low cost.[6] Our beautifully decorated model, which is located at 514 Cunningham Street, is open from[7] 10 a.m. until 7 p.m. both Saturday and Sunday. Sincerely yours, [154]

10 Dear Mrs. Stern: When we began making plans to move our company's manufacturing plant to the South last year,[1] we did not realize how many problems we would face. Frankly, if we had known how much trouble it would be to move,[2] we might have decided to remain in our old facilities.

However, now that we are located in our[3] beautiful new building and have our full staff at work, we are extremely happy. In our new location we have[4] an adequate labor supply, very good transportation facilities, and a building that should meet our needs[5] for many years to come.

I want to express my personal gratitude to your relocation company for[6] helping to make a very difficult move just a bit easier for my firm and me. Very truly yours, [139]

11 Dear Ms. Lopez: As you probably read in the newspapers recently, the Rochester Power and Light Company[1] is planning to build a new generating plant north of the city. The power plant should provide *adequate**[2] electricity for the entire area for many years to come.

On Wednesday, January 21,[3] there will be a public *hearing†* at the Madison High School auditorium. Any persons who have any[4] objections to the construction of this plant will be able to voice their opinions at that time. If you wish to[5] speak at the meeting, please fill out the enclosed form; we will add your name to the agenda for the meeting. Sincerely[6] yours, [121]

Also correct:
*enough, sufficient
†meeting

LESSON 33

4 Gentlemen: Yesterday I drove my car into your service station at 140 Third Avenue and had the[1] tank filled with lead-free gasoline. I have been using your station for the past five years, and I have never had[2] any trouble with your service or your products.

Yesterday, however, the attendant let me sit in the car for[3] a long time before he came to help me. His attitude was surly, and he acted as though I were imposing[4] on him to ask for special service. He grudgingly cleaned the windows and checked the oil, but he refused to check the[5] pressure in the tires. I asked to see the manager, but he told me that he was the only person on duty[6] at the time.

Needless to say, I was quite annoyed with the treatment I received at your station. In the future I[7] plan to take my business elsewhere. Yours truly,   [148]

5 Dear Miss Chang: I understand that the Alaska Oil Company is planning to build a new service station at[1] the intersection of Lee Street and Third Avenue, which is only a few blocks from my home. I hope that the city[2] zoning commission will take action to prevent construction of a station at this location.

At the[3] present time there are four service stations located within a three-block radius of this intersection. Formerly,[4] this was a quiet residential street. Since the service stations opened, however, several other businesses[5] have moved to the area. The street is quickly becoming a very busy commercial thoroughfare.[6]

Unless we do something soon, I fear the entire neighborhood will lose its residential character. I hope to hear[7] from you concerning this matter. Sincerely yours,   [149]

6 Dear Miss Joyce: Thank you for your willingness to help the people who live in the vicinity of Lee Street and Third[1] Avenue. We appreciate your prompt, courteous reply to our request for assistance. Needless to say, we[2] were also happy to learn that the zoning commission is monitoring the commercial development in[3] the area.

However, the residents of the community still feel that the construction of the new[4] service station is unnecessary; there are already too many service stations in the area. Regardless[5] of the type of construction, the station will add to traffic congestion. We are, therefore, filing a special[6] petition that we hope will help to prevent construction of this station. Yours truly,   [135]

7 Dear Consumer: As you know, the country has been experiencing a severe energy shortage during the[1] past few years. We here at the Commercial Oil Company want you to know that we will do our very best to[2] conserve our nation's supply of energy and to develop alternative energy sources.

During the past[3] five years, we have invested more than $30 million in research to test new sources of energy. Yet[4] we have managed to keep the cost of our gas and oil well below the average for the industry.

We are trying[5] very hard to conserve our nation's energy supply, and we hope you will do the same. There are several things that[6] you can do to help out. First, you can drive your car only when it is really necessary. Second, you can drive[7] at the posted speed limits in order to get the best mileage from each gallon of gasoline. Third, you can share[8] rides to and from work with your friends and neighbors.

Thank you for your willingness to help us help our country. Yours truly,[9]   [180]

8 Dear Ms. Case: Thank you for your letter of application for a position as an account manager with the[1] Commercial Oil Company. Your education and experience certainly seem to qualify you for the[2] special position we have open in our Mobile, Alabama, office. As you requested, we will keep your[3] application confidential.

Would it be possible for you to come to our office at 121 Main[4] Street in Mobile for a personal interview? We suggest Friday, January 30, at ten in the[5] morning.

Please let us hear from you as soon as possible. Sincerely yours,   [113]

9 Dear Mr. Jones: Thank you for your prompt reply to my letter of application for a position as an[1] account manager with the Commercial Oil Company in Mobile, Alabama. I am very *glad** that you are[2] pleased with my education and experience.

I will be happy to come to your office for a personal[3] interview on Friday, January 30. As you *suggested†*, I will be there at ten in the morning.[4]

I look forward to the interview; it will be a pleasure to meet you and your staff. Sincerely yours,   [98]

Also correct:
*happy
†asked, requested

LESSON 34

4 Dear Mr. O'Leary: If you want to keep your car running in top condition throughout the year, bring it to the[1] Pennsylvania Auto Repair Shop at 400 State Street for a general maintenance checkup. Our expert[2] mechanics will tune the motor, inspect the transmission, and make any repairs that are necessary. We will[3] give you a complete estimate of the cost of repairs before we make them. If we need to replace any[4] defective parts, we will return the old ones to you.

Just come to our State Street entrance any weekday between 7[5] a.m. and 12 noon. You don't have to make an appointment; we have more than 20 efficient mechanics who will[6] have your car ready for you when you return at 6 p.m.

Incidentally, we will fill your tank with safe,[7] dependable Pennsylvania gas, the best on the market today. We hope to see you soon. Sincerely yours,   [158]

5 Dear Miss Poland: On Wednesday, February 6, our organization, the General Power and

Light Company,[1] will hold its annual banquet for all employees, and we would like very much to have you as the speaker[2] on the program. Because of your reputation as an expert in the field of solar energy, we feel that[3] you would be an excellent person to address our group.

The meeting will be held in the Grand Ballroom of the[4] Baker Hotel. It doesn't make any difference what area of solar energy you choose for your speech; any[5] topic will be of general interest to the members of our group.

We hope you will be able to accept[6] our invitation, Miss Poland. Cordially yours, [129]

6 Dear Mr. Cunningham: It is a pleasure to write a letter of recommendation for Mr. James Garcia,[1] who has applied for a position in the personnel department of the New Hampshire Electric Company.[2] I don't know of anyone who would be better qualified for the position than he.

Mr. Garcia[3] worked for my firm from January 2, 1977, to February 10, 1979.[4] He is a person who can handle great responsibility with efficiency and dependability.[5] It doesn't matter whether the work he is assigned is easy or difficult; Mr. Garcia carries[6] it out with dispatch. He doesn't object to handling routine tasks, but he is at his best handling major[7] responsibilities.

If you hire Mr. Garcia, you will be making no mistake. Sincerely yours, [158]

7 Dear Jim: I have just received the good news that you have been named personnel director for the New Hampshire Electric[1] Company. Please accept my sincere congratulations.

From the day you first entered employment at my[2] company, I knew you had a great future. I am only sorry that you are not now working for my organization.[3]

Whenever you are in Boston, I hope you will drop in to see me. I would like to congratulate you[4] personally. Cordially yours, [86]

8 Dear Ms. Wellington: I am sure you are aware that for the past decade our nation's energy supply has been[1] shrinking. Every power company in the country has been concerned about the problem. We want you to know that[2] the Michigan Power Company has actually been doing something about it.

We realize that in perhaps[3] ten years much of our current energy supply will be depleted and that remaining reserves could prove to be[4] insufficient for the nation's demands. We have, therefore, taken several steps that will help to meet future energy[5] demands. We have stopped all exports of coal and oil. We have hired five experts to help us develop a program[6] of alternate energy supplies. We have entered into a long-term agreement with the federal government[7] in which we will work to find efficient ways to conserve our present energy resources.

You may be sure,[8] Ms. Wellington, that the Michigan Power

Company is doing everything it can to solve our nation's[9] energy problems. Sincerely yours, [186]

9 Dear Mr. Long: I was *happy** to receive your letter of Wednesday, August 4, in which you explain just what the[1] Michigan Power Company is doing to solve our nation's energy problems. I was very much impressed[2] with your program to develop alternate energy sources.

I realize, of course, that the current energy[3] supply will be insufficient for the nation's needs in the future, and it is *encouraging†* to know that[4] companies such as yours are taking major steps to solve the problem.

Congratulations on the fine work you and your[5] company are doing in this field. Sincerely yours, [110]
Also correct:
*glad, delighted
†good, nice

LESSON 35

3 *Energy To Run the World*
The world runs on energy. That goes without saying, of course, but few people actually[1] realize how dependent the world is on a variety of energy sources.

In ancient times energy[2] was supplied mainly through the use of a person's own physical strength. The power to push, pull, or lift was supplied[3] by the muscles. Even after the invention of the wheel, the main power supply was human effort. While[4] this was sufficient for a short period of time, it soon proved to be inadequate.

People quickly learned to[5] use animals as a source of power. Oxen, elephants, and eventually horses were substituted[6] to help conserve human energy.

For many years beasts of burden were the main source of power. However, it[7] was not until the discovery of fuel as a power source that humankind began to take gigantic steps[8] forward. One of the early sources of fuel power was whale oil. The whale, which was then in abundant supply, served[9] a variety of purposes. It was used for food, for heat, and even for artistic endeavors.

However,[10] it became apparent that whale oil could not forever supply the energy needs of the world. It was known[11] that eventually every whale could be killed and that there would be no more whale oil. Even in the early days[12] of the whaling industry, people began to be concerned about the whale's becoming extinct.

Some time later[13] coal became one of the world's major energy sources, and it was mined in every place practicable. In the[14] rush to supply large amounts of power, strip mining flourished. Great scars were left on the landscape throughout the world. Coal[15] was the predominant source of power for many years.

After the discovery of great oil fields from[16] Pennsylvania to Texas, this source of energy became widely used throughout the world. Oil was relatively[17] economical to refine and the supply seemed inexhaustible.

A by-product of oil was natural

gas. In[18] the early years of oil development, millions of cubic feet of natural gas were burned away. It was not[19] uncommon to see flares throughout the oil fields burning away what was then considered unusable gas. Gas,[20] however, became a major product in the years following, and ways were found to use the gas that was formerly[21] thought to be valueless.

While the world's technology advanced at a tremendously fast rate, oil supplies were[22] being depleted. Companies began to dig deeper and deeper into the earth to find adequate supplies of[23] oil and gas. Power companies even began to look under the waters of the Atlantic and Pacific[24] Oceans. It soon became apparent that the supply of oil was not inexhaustible. Major oil conservation[25] methods had to be developed, and, of course, still other sources of energy had to be found.

Now there are[26] many sources of energy being explored. There are still abundant sources of coal; however, mining the[27] coal is expensive, and there is a general concern about ecology. If coal is to be used, most[28] people believe a new method must be developed so that its burning will not pollute the atmosphere.

One of the[29] most interesting sources of energy is solar power. However, solar power is in its earliest[30] stages of actual development. It is still very expensive to use this type of power to[31] operate automobiles, to heat buildings, or to run machinery.

Yet many people believe that solar[32] power is the next major source of the world's energy supply.

Whatever source is used, it is apparent that the[33] people of the world must have abundant, clean energy in order to continue to progress.   [677]

CHAPTER 8

LESSON 36

3 Gentlemen: I am interested in purchasing a new house in Denver, where I will be moving in a few[1] months. I would like your real estate agency to help me locate a suitable house.

I need a three-bedroom house[2] with a living room, a dining room, and a den. In addition, I need an attached two-car garage. I will be[3] working in the uptown area, and I hope to find a house that is not more than an hour's commuting time[4] away. I prefer a quiet residential neighborhood with good schools, shops, and transportation.

Will you please let me[5] know the price range for a house of this type. If you would like to speak with me, my telephone number is[6] (901) 555-7244; you may call me collect. Very truly yours,   [134]

4 Dear Mr. Case: This is to acknowledge your letter of Wednesday, July 2. Thank you for considering the[1] General Real Estate Company to help you locate a home in Denver, Colorado. At the present time[2] there are a number of homes for sale in the city that I am sure will fit your needs. We should have no difficulty[3] in locating just the house that you and your family will like.

The prices range from $40,000 to[4] $95,000. The price depends on the particular area, the type of construction, and the[5] age of the house. Houses located in the northern part of the city, which is a very desirable[6] area, are priced somewhat higher than those in the other sections. However, there are good values in all areas.[7]

Brick houses are more expensive than houses of other types of construction. However, there are a number[8] of houses with aluminum siding, which provides an exterior that is relatively free of maintenance[9] problems.

When you have had an opportunity to think over the various options, please write to us. We[10] will be happy to send you detailed specifications of several available houses. Yours truly,   [219]

5 Dear Mr. Lopez: I read in yesterday morning's newspaper that you are planning to retire soon and move to[1] the South. I am wondering if you are also planning to sell your home. If you are, I hope you will list it with[2] my organization, the General Real Estate Agency. We can handle the details of the sale[3] efficiently.

My company has been in the real estate business in Maine for over ten years. We have developed a[4] reputation of dependability, efficiency, and reliability.

We can take over[5] every aspect of the sale of your house.

We first send one of our competent appraisers to your home to give you an[6] estimate of exactly what your house is worth. Then we advertise your house in the local newspapers. Only[7] when someone shows genuine interest in purchasing your house will we bring that person to see it. When we find[8] a qualified buyer for your home, we will handle all the paperwork. This, of course, includes the transfer of[9] title and insurance.

Please give us an opportunity, Mr. Lopez, to take all the worry out of selling[10] your house. Just call us or sign and return the enclosed postage-paid card; we will do the rest. Sincerely yours,   [218]

6 Dear Mr. Green: Thank you for your letter offering to handle all the details of selling my house. Your company[1] does indeed sound reliable, dependable, and efficient. I have not had any experience in[2] selling a house, and I definitely need the services of a competent real estate organization.[3]

There are several things I would like to know about your company, however, before I make a commitment to[4] you. How long would the real estate contract run? Would it be an exclusive contract, or are you a member of the[5] multiple-listing association? What fee do you charge?

When you have an opportunity, I hope you will[6] send me the answers to these questions. Sincerely yours, [130]

7 Dear Ms. White: I am happy to write a letter of recommendation for Mr. S. T. Carson, who is the[1] president of the Carson School of Real Estate.

Mr. Carson has had an account with our company for many[2] years, and he has never been late paying his bills. He is an executive of good character who handles[3] his business with responsibility and integrity.

I am glad to give Mr. Carson a good credit[4] reference. Sincerely yours, [85]

8 Dear Mr. Lopez: We were very glad to *receive** your letter stating that you are looking for a good real[1] estate firm to handle the details of selling your house. I am happy to supply the answers to your specific[2] questions.

Our standard real estate contract runs for a period of three months. We think that this is the amount of[3] time *required*† to find the right buyer for your home. The contract expires at the end of the three-month period. If[4] we have not sold your house, you have no further obligation to us. Let me assure you, however, that we will[5] do everything in our power to sell your house during that time.

We definitely prefer to have an exclusive[6] contract; in that way we have much better control of the showing of your house. We will bring prospective buyers[7] to your home only at times that are convenient for you. In addition,

you will not be bothered by five or six[8] sales representatives from different companies asking for the same information.

The standard commission[9] for selling a house in this area is 6 percent.

I am enclosing a copy of our standard contract[10] for you to read at your leisure. After you have had an opportunity to read it carefully, I hope you[11] will decide to let our organization sell your house for you. Yours very truly, [235]
Also correct:
*get
†needed

LESSON 37

5 Dear Mr. Carson: Several weeks ago I signed the preliminary papers to purchase an acre of land[1] on the corner of Jackson and Baker Streets in Wilmington, Delaware. At that time I asked that your organization[2] conduct a title search and prepare an abstract for me.

I have not heard anything from you, and I am[3] becoming quite concerned. Will you please look into this matter personally, Mr. Carson, and let me know what[4] is causing the delay. I want to sign the final papers as soon as possible, but I want to do so[5] only if the title is clear.

I hope you will let me hear from you soon. Yours truly, [114]

6 Gentlemen: I hope to purchase two duplexes that are located at 274 and 275[1] Main Street in Richmond, Virginia. I have

chosen this property because it is located in a quiet[2] suburban neighborhood. Prior to signing the final papers, however, I want the houses to have a thorough[3] inspection.

I want to have the roofs inspected for wind, rain, or hail damage. I want to have the wood checked for[4] any evidence of termites. In addition, I want to have the electrical systems and the plumbing[5] inspected throughout the houses.

Are you interested in doing this work for me? If you are, I hope you will get in[6] touch with me as soon as possible. I want to have the inspection made within the next one or two weeks so that[7] I can make a final decision on the purchase of the property. Yours truly,   [155]

7 Dear Mr. Case: Did you know that the price of real estate in South Carolina has risen an average of[1] 10 percent in each of the past three years? Did you know that an investment in real estate is a safer, more[2] economical investment than any other type of savings program available to you in today's[3] market?

If you have not considered these things, I hope you will take a few minutes to look over the enclosed brochure.[4] It outlines briefly the various types of real estate currently available in Charleston and Columbia.[5] The person who has $10,000, $20,000, or $30,000 to invest at[6] this time can easily get a return of 10 percent per annum by purchasing real estate.

Whether you wish[7] to buy undeveloped land, finished houses, or industrial buildings, real estate is the wisest investment[8] today. Decide today to quit risking your valuable savings in an uncertain stock market. Write to us for[9] more information. Sincerely yours,   [187]

8 Dear Mr. Mason: Thank you for writing to me about the future of Bryant Park. The members of the planning[1] commission are always very glad to hear from interested citizens with regard to any public[2] project.

Some time ago we began looking for ways to *cut** the expenses of operating Bryant Park. As you[3] know, there are no restaurant facilities in the vicinity, and we *feel†* that a good restaurant would make[4] an excellent addition to the park. We are now considering leasing a two-square block area within[5] Bryant Park to a commercial restaurant. The area under consideration is on the eastern side[6] of the park and has never been fully utilized. It was once used as a parking lot, but the city quit[7] using it several years ago. Very few people even realize that it is actually a part of the park.

The[8] National Restaurant Association has made a generous offer to develop the complete area.[9] They will provide a large parking area that can be used by all park visitors at any time the[10] restaurant is not open. The revenue derived from the restaurant will finance nearly 40 percent of the[11] operating expenses of the entire park.

Under the circumstances, I hope you will understand why the[12] members of the planning commission feel that this is quite a good investment for the city. Sincerely yours, [259]

Also correct:
*reduce
†think, believe

LESSON 38

4 Dear Dr. Taylor: If you are looking for a new home, we have a suggestion for you. Invest in a beautiful[1] new home in Greenville County.

Here is some information that we believe will be of interest to you.[2] Greenville County is located only 25 miles from the heart of the city; however, it is worlds away[3] in terms of cost, convenience, and atmosphere. In Greenville County you will find hundreds of new homes ranging in price[4] from $50,000 to over $100,000. Two new interstate highways serve the county;[5] it is one of the most accessible areas in the entire region. In addition, there are three train[6] stations in convenient locations for those commuters who do not want to drive their cars into the city.

Make[7] arrangements to visit Greenville County soon; we know you will like it. Sincerely yours, [154]

5 Dear Mr. Sweet: We are delighted to inform you that your application for a loan to purchase a new home[1] at 411 34th Street in Greenville County has been approved.

We have checked your credit references, and[2] in our judgment you are an excellent credit risk. In addition, we feel that the location of the house you[3] have selected is an unusually good one.

If you will drop by the bank any day next week between the hours[4] of 9 a.m. and 5 p.m., we will have the final mortgage papers ready for you to sign. You do not need[5] an appointment.

Congratulations, Mr. Sweet, on your decision to purchase a new home. We know you will[6] enjoy it for many years to come. Sincerely yours, [129]

6 Ladies and Gentlemen: I am looking for a new location for my management office somewhere near the[1] center of Jackson, Mississippi, where I will be moving sometime during the next three or four months. If your real[2] estate agency has any buildings available that meet my specific needs, I hope you will let me hear from[3] you.

If it is possible, I want to purchase a large building that will serve both residential and vocational[4] purposes. I need a two- or three-floor house with two separate entrances.

On the first floor I want to install[5] my business management office. On the second and third floors I want to have my living quarters. In the living[6] area I will need three bedrooms, a living room, a kitchen, and two bathrooms.

If you have any buildings that[7] you think would serve my needs, please send me photographs and complete information about them. Sincerely yours, [158]

7 Dear Ms. Park: Thank you for your prompt reply to my request for information about homes in Jackson, Mississippi.¹ I am very much impressed with the descriptions and photographs of the three houses that you mailed to me. If² the houses are as well constructed as they appear to be, I am sure that one of them will serve very well as³ a place for me to work and live in Jackson.

If it is possible, please make arrangements for me to see each of⁴ the three houses on Saturday, February 21. I will be flying to the Jackson area that⁵ morning and will be there until Monday morning, February 23. Will you please let me know as soon as⁶ possible if you can make these arrangements. Sincerely yours, [131]

8 Dear Mr. Brown: It was a real pleasure to meet you this past weekend during your short visit to our city. I¹ am happy that the Dependable Real Estate Agency was able to help you find a building that will serve² your office and residential needs. I am sorry that the location is not in the middle of the city,³ but I am sure that you will find the north side an excellent neighborhood in which to live and work.

As I pointed⁴ out to you, the building you chose will not be available until March 15. The owner, Mrs. Betty⁵ Edwards, feels that she needs the time

until that date to vacate the premises.

In the meantime, I am making arrangements⁶ for the transfer of title. Sincerely yours, [129]

9 Dear Ms. Park: Several months ago I decided to move to Jackson, Mississippi. I asked your *organization*¹* to help me find a suitable place to establish my management office. From the first contact with your² company, I found your service to be excellent.

The office staff treated me with respect and courtesy. When I³ found a building in a desirable location, your staff handled all the paperwork easily, quickly, and⁴ efficiently.

I have now begun my management work in Jackson, and my family is well established in⁵ the *community*.† I wanted to write a note to tell you how much I appreciated your fine service.⁶ Sincerely yours, [122]

Also correct:
*company, agency
†city, neighborhood

LESSON 39

4 Gentlemen: My organization, the Jennings Oil Company, is planning to lease office space in Baltimore,¹ Maryland, in the near future. We are wondering whether your realty company would like to handle the² details for us.

We will need between 20,000 and 30,000 square feet of office space in a modern³ office building near all transportation facilities. The building should have up-to-date heating and air-conditioning[4] facilities. In addition, we want to have adequate parking inside the building for at least[5] 100 cars.

Do you have any listings that will meet our needs? If you do, will you please get in touch with me as soon[6] as possible. You can reach me between the hours of nine and five Monday through Friday at (209) 555-4101.[7] Sincerely yours,   [143]

5 Dear Mrs. Stern: For the past year my associates and I have been considering transferring our envelope[1] manufacturing plant to the South. For many years we have been very well satisfied with our present location,[2] but our company has become too large for our present facilities.

It is not possible for us to[3] expand our current building, and the nearest suitable location in the area is more than 50 miles[4] away. If we should move just 50 miles, we are sure that we would lose almost all of our present work force. We are,[5] therefore, considering relocating to an area where the weather is warmer.

I understand that your[6] organization can help us find a good location and assist us in the many things we must do to make this[7] move. If you would like to discuss the job with members of our management staff and me, please call us soon. Sincerely[8] yours,   [161]

6 Dear Mr. Kennedy: Your company is facing one of the most difficult times in its history. When the management[1] of a company decides that it must move from one state to another, there are literally[2] thousands of problems that arise. You made no mistake, Mr. Kennedy, when you chose the Madison Relocation[3] Company to assist you in your move.

Our staff of more than 25 well-trained employees will help you find a[4] suitable location in an area where there is an ample labor supply, where the local tax structure[5] is favorable to your type of business, and where there are adequate transportation facilities. In[6] addition, we will help you with all the details of transferring those members of your present staff who wish to move to[7] the South with your company.

If you want to discuss all the services that we offer, I suggest that you meet[8] with my staff and me soon. Please tell me a time that will be convenient for you. Cordially yours,   [177]

7 Dear Mr. Pack: We received your advertising letter stating that your company provides relocation[1] services for company employees who are transferred from one *city** to another.

Because we have several[2] employees who will be transferred to our Los Angeles, California, office within the next three or four months, we[3] believe that your company may be able to *offer*† substantial help to us.

Will you please let us know exactly[4] what the cost would be to help us find suitable homes for three families in the Los Angeles area.[5] We want to assist these families in finding homes, in making arrangements for moving their furniture and[6] personal belongings, and in getting acquainted with their new neighborhood. Sincerely yours, [136]

Also correct:
*area, state
†give, render

LESSON 40

3 *Investing in Real Estate*

When it comes to investing, some people feel that real estate is the best place for their[1] money. They believe that real estate represents a safer, better investment than stocks or bonds. In some cases[2] this may be true, but in others it definitely is not.

It is true, of course, that real estate generally[3] increases in value over the years. However, not every investment in real estate pays big dividends.[4] Some people have made as much as 20 percent or 30 percent profit in one year on a real estate[5] investment. However, a great many others have not been able to realize even a small profit after[6] many years.

Investing in real estate does have a number of advantages for the wise investor. First, taxes[7] that are paid on domestic real estate are deductible for most income tax purposes. For the homeowner[8] this can mean big savings each year. For example, if a homeowner pays $1,000, $2,000,[9] or even $3,000 during the course of a year in real estate taxes, this amount may be deducted[10] from gross income before determining the amount of income tax that must be paid.

Another advantage[11] of investing in real estate is that interest on money borrowed to finance the purchase may also be[12] deducted from gross income before determining taxes. This is true, of course, of interest on money[13] borrowed to finance any type of purchase. However, people seldom think of borrowing money to make[14] other types of investments.

Over the past few years real estate has appreciated in value faster than most[15] other types of assets. This means that while money invested in a savings account might realize a return of[16] only 6 percent or 7 percent, a person might make 10 percent or 15 percent on a real estate[17] investment. In addition, the net amount gained in a year's time is taxed in a different manner that quite often[18] favors the real estate investor.

But the picture in real estate investment is not always bright. Seldom does[19] anyone make a fortune overnight in any type of business, and real estate is no exception. The[20] unwary buyer may be encouraged to invest in property located in a faraway state. Often[21] prospective purchasers are induced to make an investment in property that they have never even seen. When the[22] buyer eventually sees the property, it may prove to be worthless. It may be located in the middle[23] of a desert, near a swamp, or on the side of a mountain. In such cases the only people who make overnight[24] profits are those who sell the worthless property. Many state governments are becoming increasingly[25] concerned about this type of business operation. They report that they now have regulations governing the sale[26] of such land.

Before making an investment in real estate, it is best to think the matter over carefully[27] to determine if that is the best type of investment to make. One should read every available report[28] about the area where the property is located. One must attempt to find answers to many questions. Is[29] the property located in a desirable area? Are there such conveniences as access to public[30] transportation? Are public utilities available? Are the taxes reasonable? Is the area[31] likely to increase in value, or is there reason to believe that it will decrease substantially over the[32] years?

An investment in real estate can be good, or it can be bad. It can return great dividends, or it can[33] be a financial burden. The wise investor must make decisions based on facts and not rely on opinions.[34]   [680]

CHAPTER 9

LESSON 41

4 Dear Mr. Short: I am sure you are aware of the constantly rising prices in most food stores. The management[1] here at General Food Stores is keenly aware that the price of food has risen more than 6 percent during the[2] past year. Yet we are making a definite effort to hold the line on food prices. We are searching daily for[3] better wholesale buys in order to pass any savings that we make on to our customers.

Even with our[4] very best efforts, however, we know that we will not be able to stop inflation. Nevertheless, you may be[5] sure that we will do everything in our power to keep prices at the lowest level possible. Stop by[6] your nearest General Food Store, which is located at 400 Worth Street, and see for yourself what we are[7] doing to keep our prices low. Yours truly,   [147]

5 Dear Mrs. O'Neill: For many years I have been a loyal customer of the Eastern Food Store on Main Street. I[1] have found your store to offer first-class food products at competitive prices.

During the past few months, however,[2] I have become increasingly aware that the quality of goods at your store has deteriorated[3] badly. The meats are substandard, and the fruits and vegetables are often stale. In addition, I have found that the[4] bakery products are dry and tasteless.

Frankly, I am perplexed. I cannot understand why the quality of your[5] products has dropped; the prices have continued to rise. If the quality does not improve in the next few days, I[6] will certainly take my business to one of your competitors. Yours truly,   [134]

6 Dear Consumer: We are beginning something new here at the Modern Supermarket at 142 Park Street.[1] We are instituting an entirely new way of selling groceries.

On the 1st of November we will[2] discontinue selling small quantities of goods; instead, we will sell only in large, family-sized containers. We[3] will no longer employ special people to place the items you purchase in bags or to carry them to your car.[4] Prices will not be marked on individual items; the prices will appear only on the shelves below the[5] products.

Why are we doing these things? We are instituting this new program to help you cut your food costs. We believe[6] that we can help you save as much as 15 percent on your food bill. Come in November 1 and see for yourself[7] how much you can save with our new method. Sincerely yours,

[150]

7 Dear Miss Pack: When I saw your advertisement in the newspaper a few weeks ago, I was particularly[1] glad to know that your grocery store is making a serious attempt to help the people of our community[2] lower their food bills.

I went to your store the first week after you had converted to the new bulk-quantity[3] system. I did not mind buying in large, economy-sized packages. I did not mind carrying my own bags[4] to the car. However, I do not like the idea of eliminating the price from each individual[5] item. Plac-

ing the price only on the shelf can cause problems. Several times I was not sure exactly which price[6] applied to the product I wanted to buy.

I want you to know, Miss Pack, that in general I like the new method,[7] but I hope you will reinstate the policy of placing a price on each item. Sincerely yours,

[158]

8 Dear Mr. Flynn: Thank you very much for your letter of Thursday, December 10. I was particularly *glad**[1] to receive it because we are definitely interested in the opinions of our regular customers.[2] We had hoped, of course, that our new system of selling food products would be accepted, but we were not sure[3] exactly how the public would *like*†it.

I am happy to say that the majority of our customers like the[4] system very much. However, many of them agree with you that the prices of individual items[5] should be placed on the packages. We are, therefore, returning to our old policy of marking each item[6] individually.

Thank you, Mr. Flynn, for your patronage over the years; we are looking forward to seeing you[7] in our store often in the future. Sincerely yours,   [150]

Also correct:
*happy, delighted
†accept, react to

LESSON 42

4 Dear Mr. Smith: As manager of the Mason Food Store in Provo,

Utah, you will be very glad to know that[1] on the 15th of August the Mason food chain will begin its changeover to unit pricing in all stores. In addition[2] to the regular price that is marked on each item, the price per unit will be marked on the shelf. In this[3] way consumers will be able to compare the actual price per unit of any product that they wish to[4] purchase.

We will begin our program in our main store here in Cleveland, Ohio, in August. During the month of[5] September we will institute unit pricing in our stores in Washington, Montana, and Utah. Each month[6] thereafter we will proceed by adding two or three more states until we have completed the project.

We will keep you[7] posted on our progress. Sincerely yours, [147]

5 Dear Miss Wilson: The residents of the eastern section of Cincinnati, Ohio, are planning a new[1] program in which I believe you will be interested. More than 500 men and women met last week and decided[2] to form a food cooperative. By using a cooperative, we believe that we will be able to make[3] substantial savings on our food bills.

Several of our members will go to the wholesale food markets each morning and[4] purchase large quantities of items that the cooperative members ordinarily buy on the retail[5] level. We will operate a small store of our own in which only members may make purchases. The members will pay[6] a fee of $5 each month and will serve as buyers once every month. We will have only one full-time employee,[7] the person who operates the store.

If you would like to enroll in this program, which is unique in our[8] area, please let us hear from you as soon as possible. Sincerely yours, [173]

6 Dear Members: We are happy to report that the food cooperative we started last year has finished its first full[1] year of operation in very good shape.

We now have over 1,000 members who shop regularly with[2] us, and we expect another 100 to enter the program soon. We can say that our members have saved[3] about $100,000 on their food bills during the year. Our procedures are working well, and only on[4] one or two occasions have we had complaints about our service from our members.

We hope that there will be even[5] greater progress in the coming year. If you have any particular suggestions that you feel will help us[6] better our service, we hope you will let us hear from you soon. Cordially yours, [133]

7 Dear Mrs. Chang: I was very glad to learn from our mutual friend, J. D. Casey, that you have just been promoted[1] to the position of general manager of the State Street Food Store in Lynn, Massachusetts. Congratulations[2] on your wonderful new job; you certainly deserve it.

When you first entered employment with the White Food Chain,[3] which owns the State Street Food

Store, I predicted great things for you. You are one of the best employees that the company[4] has ever had. I now predict even better things for you. I would not be surprised if you were made a[5] district or regional manager in the future.

When your busy schedule will allow it, I hope you will take time[6] to have lunch with me. I would like to congratulate you in person. Cordially yours,   [135]

8 Dear Ms. Grimes: On Saturday, April 8, the residents of Cleveland will have an unusual opportunity.[1] On that date we will be able to hear one of the most outstanding speakers in the nation. Ms. Mary White,[2] who has represented Cleveland in the state government in Columbus and in the federal government in[3] Washington, will be the guest speaker at the regular spring meeting of the Ohio Food Distributors[4] Association.

The meeting will be held in the Hotel Smith. There will be a formal reception for Ms. White in[5] the Blue Room, which is near the main entrance to the hotel on Pennsylvania Avenue. The reception will be[6] followed by a dinner in the main dining room. Ms. White will make her presentation in the same room immediately[7] following the dinner. The topic of her talk will be things we can do to contribute to the success of[8] our state association.

I suggest, Ms. Grimes, that you make your reservation for this particular meeting[9] as early as possible. I feel sure that once the news is out that Ms. White will be our guest speaker, we will have[10] more people who wish to attend the meeting than we can possibly accept. Sincerely yours,
[217]

9 Dear Mr. Poland: How nice it was to see you again last week. I *certainly** enjoyed talking over old times[1] with you. It doesn't seem possible that it has been more than ten years since we began working together for the[2] White Food Chain.

Thank you for the *wonderful†* lunch at the Johnson Restaurant; the food was delicious. However, it[3] was your company that made the occasion a memorable one for me.

When you are again in this area,[4] I hope you will stop by to see me. Sincerely yours,   [90]
Also correct:
*really, truly
†excellent, fine

LESSON 43

4 Dear Mr. Torres: Several days ago I read in the newspaper that you are planning to open a new[1] restaurant in the Western Shopping Mall in Spokane, Washington. If you have not already equipped your new building,[2] I am sure you will be interested in what our company can do for you. My organization, Stern, Lee,[3] and Company, has been in the restaurant supply business in Washington for over ten years. We sell dishes,[4] cooking utensils, and various other supplies that are necessary in any restaurant.

I am[5] enclosing a complete catalog listing all our supplies. Please note particularly the wide variety of[6] dishes shown beginning on page 42. As you will see, we offer all types of dishes from basic plastic[7] cups, which are used in many restaurants, to classic china, which is ordinarily used in private homes.[8] Whatever your preference may be, I am sure you will find just what you need in our catalog.

We hope to hear from you[9] soon. Sincerely yours,   [184]

5 Dear Miss Jefferson: Two years ago I opened a restaurant in the Western Shopping Mall in Spokane. At that[1] time the public accepted the new business very well. We served more than 300 people on an average day.[2] However, recently our business has dropped off drastically.

At the present time we are serving no more than[3] 100 people on an average day. We have taken specific steps to try to regain our customers, but we[4] have not been able to do so. Because of budgetary reasons, we now find it necessary to take a[5] number of additional steps.

Before I make any major changes in the operation of the restaurant,[6] however, I would like to discuss the matter with someone from your consulting firm. Will you please ask one of[7] your representatives to visit me as soon as possible. I hope that your organization will be[8] able to recommend several possible solutions to my problem. Yours truly,   [174]

6 Dear Mr. Torres: Thank you for writing me about the problems you are having with the operation of[1] your restaurant in Spokane. My consulting firm will be glad to work with you and help you effect a speedy[2] resolution to your problem.

The basic problem that many restaurant owners face in today's market is that[3] shoppers want high-quality food prepared very quickly and sold at low prices. They no longer consider the[4] amenities of a fine restaurant necessary in the middle of a fast-paced shopping day. This probably[5] applies in your case too.

A number of fine restaurants are being converted to a fast-food type of[6] operation. Some are succeeding; some are failing. It all depends on the basic character of the neighborhood[7] in which the restaurant is located and the manner in which the restaurant is operated.

Our firm has[8] helped a number of financially pressed companies turn their operations around in only a short time. I[9] am sure we will be able to do the same thing for you.

I would like to suggest that we have a conference[10] concerning your problems at 9 a.m. on Wednesday, July 6, at my office at 410 Main Street. Please call my[11] secretary, Ms. Lee Smith, at 555-1401 to confirm the appointment. Sincerely yours,   [238]

7 Dear Mr. White: As you probably know, the City Council of Medford recently enacted a new law that[1] applies to the regulation of the operation of all the city's restaurants. The law concerns such[2] basic items as sanitary conditions in the kitchen, the health of all employees, and the maximum[3] number of customers that the restaurant may serve at one time. Each restaurant in the city will be checked at least[4] once a year to be sure that it complies with all the regulations.

The first visit to your restaurant will be[5] on Monday, June 2. Our team of inspectors will arrive sometime in the morning and complete the inspection[6] within an hour's time. After the initial visit, your restaurant may be visited again at any time[7] without prior notification.

We know you understand the basic reasons for such inspections, Mr. White,[8] and we appreciate your cooperation in this matter. Yours truly,   [174]

8 Dear Mr. Jones: This letter is in reference to the recent inspection of your restaurant at 140[1] Glenville Street. We are very sorry to tell you that your restaurant failed to meet the city's new regulations that[2] apply to all restaurants.

There are two basic problems in your restaurant. There are 100 tables; there is[3] adequate space for only 75. In addition, three of your employees do not have cards *indicating*[4] they have had physical examinations.

You have one week in which to correct these specific violations.[5] If you have not complied with the law by the end of a week, your restaurant will be closed. We

know, Mr. Jones,[6] that you want to comply with the city regulations. We expect to find your restaurant in *good*[†] condition[7] when we see you again next week. Yours truly,   [148]
Also correct:
*stating, showing
†excellent, top

LESSON 44

4 Dear Mr. Smith: The Better Business Club of Helena, Montana, would like to invite your company, the[1] Western Food Store, to become a member of our organization.

As you probably know, the Better Business Club[2] is composed of over 300 business executives of Helena who are dedicated to improving[3] business relationships in the city. We are a self-regulating organization that monitors[4] all types of business practices. We provide services not only for our own membership but also for the[5] public in general. We know that honest business practices further business and that unscrupulous business[6] dealings hurt everyone.

The majority of the people throughout the city recognize the Better Business Club[7] emblem on the doors of all our member organizations. If you would like to join our organization, you[8] may submit your application by completing the enclosed self-addressed application form. We will be happy[9] to receive it. Sincerely yours,   [186]

5 Dear Miss Chang: Thank you very much for your invitation to become a member of the Better Business Club of[1] Helena. I am delighted to accept. The integrity and ideals of your organization suit me[2] perfectly; they are consistent with the way in which I strive to operate my food store. I try to give top-quality[3] goods and services and make a reasonable profit in return.

I am submitting my formal[4] application with this letter. I look forward to being a member of your organization. Yours truly, [99]

6 Ladies and Gentlemen: On Friday and Saturday, February 3 and 4, my organization, the[1] Southern Food Company, will be holding its annual management meeting in Charleston, South Carolina. We would[2] like to reserve a number of rooms at your hotel to accommodate our staff.

We will need ten single rooms for[3] both evenings and a large suite of two or three rooms for our business meetings. Each room in the suite should be equipped with[4] a table and four chairs.

If you can accommodate us, please let me know as soon as possible. Yours truly, [99]

7 Dear Mrs. Carson: A woman by the name of Ms. Sylvia Garcia has submitted her application[1] for a job as an executive secretary with the General Food Company, and she has listed you[2] as a reference. Will you please take a few minutes to give us your opinion of Ms. Garcia.

We are looking[3] for a person who is self-reliant and self-confident. We need someone who can handle substantial amounts[4] of work without direct supervision. In addition, we need a person of great integrity who can work[5] with highly confidential information.

If you will let us have your opinion of Ms. Garcia, you will[6] have our gratitude. If we can ever return the favor, we will be very glad to do so. Sincerely yours,[7] [140]

8 Dear Mrs. Harrington: We are happy to announce the opening of our new restaurant in the Birmingham[1] Shopping Center. On the evening of Saturday, February 4, we will have our formal opening.

We will,[2] of course, continue to operate our fine restaurant at 432 21st Avenue, and we want[3] to continue our wonderful relationships with our customers who have been loyal to us over the years[4] at that location.

However, we want to make many new friendships in our new location. Therefore, during the[5] first week of operation in the Birmingham Shopping Center, we will offer everything on our menu at[6] one-half the regular price. We hope you will plan to spend a memorable evening with us soon. Sincerely yours,[7] [140]

9 Dear Miss Jennings: One of the things that make a restaurant distinctive is the appearance of the employees. The[1] public image of a restaurant is substantially improved if the employees are dressed neatly. Our company[2] can supply your restaurant with tailored suits for both men and women. We sell formal clothing, casual wear,[3] and regular uniforms of all types.

We would like to send you a copy of our circular that shows the wide[4] variety of uniforms we have to offer. Just fill out and *return**the enclosed card. We will send you the[5] circular by return mail. We are sure, Miss Jennings, that we have *exactly*† the type of clothing that will suit your[6] needs perfectly. Yours truly,   [125]
Also correct:
*mail
†just

LESSON 45

3 *Franchising Food*
Over the years the restaurant business has changed radically. Many old restaurants have[1] suffered loss of business; however, others have flourished. The restaurants that have gained the greatest number of customers[2] in recent years are fast-food establishments. Just what do we mean when we talk about the fast-food business? We[3] are usually talking about a clean, neatly decorated restaurant that is designed for quick service from[4] an extremely limited menu. Fast-food restaurants are often located at major traffic intersections[5] or in major shopping centers. Many of the establishments are franchise operations.

A franchised[6] restaurant has several advantages. First, expert managers help the new owner get the business started. Second,[7] standard signs help the public to recognize the restaurant immediately. Third, national advertising[8] helps the new business gain public acceptance very quickly.

Franchise restaurants often develop loyal[9] customers over an entire geographic area. For example, a traveling business executive[10] may look for the familiar sign of a favorite fast-food restaurant before stopping for lunch or dinner.[11] People have come to expect a set standard for both food and service at franchise restaurants. In fact, the employees[12] of one particularly successful franchise restaurant spend several weeks' time in school learning exactly[13] how to prepare the food and how to operate the restaurant.

A company that sells franchises often sends[14] management teams to inspect restaurants in its chain. These teams check the quality of the food, the speed of service,[15] and the general attitude of the employees. Those restaurants that do not meet the standards are issued a[16] warning that they must correct any deficiencies within a short period of time.

Franchise restaurants are[17] owned and operated by independent business executives who are responsible for the successful[18] operation of their businesses. If a problem develops, however, the franchise company is ordinarily[19] available for consultation. Chances are very good that the company can solve the problem[20] quickly.

Many franchise restaurants have automated ordering systems. An employee takes an order and[21] simply checks the items wanted with a magnetic pencil on a special order form. The form is then put[22] into an electronic device that prints out the order, totals the bill, and can even tell how much change is due the[23] customer. The actual order is processed almost as efficiently. An assembly line of employees[24] prepares the order quickly and easily.

In a fast-food restaurant customers usually stand in line to[25] place their orders and carry their own food to the tables. When the customers have finished eating, they are encouraged[26] by large signs to carry their trays to the cleaning area.

Fast-food restaurants ordinarily serve food in[27] paper or disposable plastic containers. Many restaurants have found that using these types of containers is[28] less expensive than washing regular dishes. However, a few restaurants have switched back to glass or[29] durable plastic dishes in order to conserve natural resources. Those that continue to use disposable[30] containers are encouraged to recycle their used paper and plastic containers.

The success of the franchise[31] food business is based on the ability of the restaurant to serve consistently good food rapidly and[32] at reasonable prices. In the future, public tastes may change; however, it appears that the future of[33] the fast-food business is secure.   [666]

4 Learning To Cook

Many years ago learning to cook was a task that took a great deal of time. In fact, in some countries[1] a young boy or girl might become an apprentice to a master chef for a period of many years. During[2] that time the apprentice would work long, difficult hours and receive little or no money. However, the[3] apprentice would gain knowledge and skill every day. When the apprenticeship was completed, the young person could take a[4] position with a major restaurant and command a large salary and great respect.

In modern times the practice[5] of learning to be a chef by apprenticeship has almost disappeared. However, cooking schools are becoming[6] increasingly popular. Many major department stores offer short courses for those people who want to[7] learn to cook special types of foods. Some colleges and universities actually offer courses in food[8] preparation. But the majority of people still learn basic cooking while they are youngsters watching their mothers,[9] fathers, or other relatives prepare food.

To some people food preparation is an interesting, challenging[10] job. To others it is dull, routine work. To still others it represents a fascinating hobby.

There will always[11] be positions for people who like to prepare food and who have learned to do it well. Learning to cook can be[12] a rewarding experience in terms of both money and personal satisfaction.   [256]

CHAPTER 10

LESSON 46

3 Dear Mr. O'Keefe: If you are operating your business with old-fashioned mechanical office machines while[1] your competitors are using new, modern computers, you are probably losing valuable business. It is[2] common knowledge that the most successful companies today are making full use of all the capabilities[3] of advanced computer technology.

Many business executives feel that the cost of installing a[4] computer would be prohibitive. Actually, not having a computer may be a great deal more costly to your[5] company's success. Let one of our expert representatives come to your office soon to explain to you in[6] detail just what one of our electronic computers can do for your business. Call us today at[7] 555-1671 for an appointment; you will be glad you did. Sincerely yours, [154]

4 Dear Miss Lexington: Do you know that you can have all the advantages of a computer in your office[1] without the expense of purchasing one? Yes, you can take advantage of the electronic marvels that computer[2] technology affords simply by installing a computer terminal in your office.

For a one-time[3] installation fee and a moderate service charge each month thereafter, you can use one of the world's largest computers.[4] The computer itself will not be in your office, of course. It will stay in our main office building in[5] Chicago, Illi-nois, but you will have access to it any time you wish.

Whenever you want to use the computer,[6] you simply type a special code number, which we will assign to you, on the terminal keyboard. Then you[7] enter new information into the computer memory or call up any information you need. You will have[8] immediate access to information that ordinarily might take as long as several hours' time to[9] obtain.

One of our factory-trained representatives will be glad to come to your office to discuss in detail[10] with you all the advantages of installing a computer terminal in your office. Just fill out, sign, and[11] return the enclosed card. When we receive it, we will set up an appointment at a time that will be convenient[12] for you. Yours truly, [244]

5 Dear Mr. Evans: I have just returned from a very difficult business trip, which was made a great deal easier[1] by your airline. I wanted to take a moment to tell you how much I appreciate the fine service your[2] employees provided me.

Due to extremely bad weather conditions in the East, I was delayed for several[3] hours at the air terminal in Philadelphia. The delay caused me to miss a connecting flight in Pittsburgh.[4] When I did not check in for the second leg of my flight, the entire remainder of my trip was canceled through a[5] computer error. Needless to say, I was very much upset.

However, one of your representatives helped[6] me reschedule the flights and even found an alternate air route to my final destination, Cleveland, Ohio.[7] The representative did this even though the flight was on another airline. Another of your[8] representatives located my baggage and transferred it to the new airline.

The result was that I was on time for[9] a very important business meeting. It is this type of service, Mr. Evans, that has won your airline so[10] many friends over the years. Thanks for making travel easier for me. Sincerely yours, [216]

6 Dear Miss Schultz: This is to acknowledge your recent letter. Thank you very much for your invitation for Mr.[1] James Harvey to speak at your company's sales meeting on Thursday, April 2. Mr. Harvey is away from[2] the office on an extended business trip; he will not return until November 1.

At the present time[3] Mr. Harvey's *calendar** is quite full, but he might be able to accept your invitation if he can adjust[4] his schedule. However, we will not be able to give you a *definite†* answer until after November[5] 1.

You may be sure, Miss Schultz, that Mr. Harvey will be corresponding with you then. Sincerely yours, [118]
Also correct:
*schedule
†final

LESSON 47

5 Dear Mr. Gordon: In the mail today we received your letter asking us to close your charge account with the San[1] Antonio Department Store. Needless to say, your letter disturbed us greatly. A quick check of our computer[2] printout shows that for the past three or four years you have been one of our best customers. During that time we have tried[3] to provide you with high-quality goods and services. You have used your charge account regularly and have paid[4] your bills promptly each month.

But something must be wrong. Perhaps we have done something to offend you. Perhaps we have not[5] done something you wanted us to do. Perhaps you have not received the service to which you are entitled.

Whatever[6] the real problem is, we want to keep you as a regular customer in the future. However, we will[7] not know what to do if you do not tell us what the problem is. Will you please take a few minutes' time to write a[8] short reply on the back of this letter to let us know exactly what the trouble is. We hope to hear from you[9] soon. Sincerely yours, [184]

6 Dear Ms. White: Thank you very much for writing to me personally about my closing my charge account with the[1] San Antonio Department Store. Frankly, it is the first real contact I have had with a member of the[2] management of your company in the past three years.

As you noted, I have used my charge account regularly[3] during the past four years, and I have paid my bills promptly. However, two or three times each year there have been computer[4] errors on my monthly statements. Each time it has taken at least three or four weeks to correct the error. The[5] problems were eventually solved, but it has taken a great deal of time and effort. As a result, I have come to[6] the conclusion that it would be much easier for me to pay cash for my purchases at your store.

I have[7] always considered the San Antonio Department Store one of the best in the area, and I do not[8] intend to stop buying things there. However, in the future my shopping will be done on a cash basis. Yours truly,[9] [180]

7 Dear Mrs. Taylor: If you have ever lost valuable computer programs because they were stored on poor-quality[1] tape, you know the real value of high-quality computer tape. General computer tape is made of the[2] best materials and is treated so that it will give years of worry-free service.

General tape costs a[3] little more than regular computer tape, but it is worth much more. The enclosed circular shows our complete line of[4] computer tapes and their prices. As you will notice, the tapes come in both eight-inch reels and ten-inch reels. The reels will[5] fit any standard computer.

Do not wait until you lose a set of valuable records; transfer all important[6] work to General computer tape now. If you have any questions concerning our products, just write us at[7] our El Paso, Texas, office. Sincerely yours,
[149]

8 Dear Mr. Anderson: Several months ago I was in your leather goods store in Orlando, Florida, and I[1] purchased a suede jacket. When I returned to my home in Tampa, I realized that the jacket had a three-inch tear[2] in the left sleeve. I immediately returned the jacket to your store, and I received a letter of[3] apology from a clerk in your office.

However, for the past two months I have received bills for the jacket. The bills,[4] of course, are incorrect, but I have not been able to get anyone in your office to make the proper computer[5] entry to remove the charge from my account.

I do not wish to be unreasonable, but I must[6] insist that something be done immediately. Will you please take care of this problem yourself, Mr. Anderson.[7] Sincerely yours, [142]

9 Dear Miss Lee: Thank you for writing to us about the *problem** you have had getting the charge for the leather jacket[1] that you returned to us removed from your bill. It seems that everyone in the store understood the problem perfectly.[2] However, we somehow failed to convey the message to our computer. I just made the *proper*† computer[3] entry myself; I should have done so two months ago.

I am enclosing our circular that describes our new line[4] of fall fashions. As I am sure you expect, we have a full line of the latest, most up-to-date fashions in both[5] real leather and fine handmade fabrics.

We hope to see you again in our store in the near future. Cordially yours,[6]   [120]
Also correct:
*trouble
†right, actual, correct

LESSON 48

4 Gentlemen: Sometime in the next few months our organization is planning to expand its offices, which are[1] located at 712 West 87 Street in Odessa, Texas. We have experienced great growth in[2] our business during the past ten years, and we find that our office facilities are no longer[3] adequate.

To solve our immediate problems, we plan to add at least 10,000 square feet of floor space and to[4] install a new records-retention system. At the time of the expansion we also plan to replace our[5] present computer with a new, much larger one.

Your company has been recommended to us as one of the[6] leaders in the field of computers. Would you be interested in submitting a bid on a new computer for[7] my company? If you would, will you please ask one of your representatives to call me sometime during the next[8] week to make an appointment to discuss this matter. Sincerely yours, [173]

5 Dear Mr. Mason: It was very nice to meet you and your personnel on my recent visit to your company.[1] I have seldom seen such a well-run office. It will be a pleasure to work with you on the installation[2] of a new computer system for your company.

You will be pleased to know that our preliminary survey[3] indicates that our Model 21 computer will be adequate to meet the needs of your company now[4] and for many years in the future. The Model 21 is a compact unit finished in a light gray[5] exterior that will blend into your present office color scheme. This model complies with all government[6] regulations for safety and economy of operation.

You may purchase the machine, or if you wish to[7] avoid a large initial expenditure, you may lease it. We recommend that one of our engineers be on site[8] while you are remodeling your offices to help plan the electrical wiring necessary for the[9] machine.

We know, Mr. Mason, that you will be pleased with the Model 21 computer, with our staff, and with the[10] service we give you. Yours truly,   [206]

6 Dear Mr. Strong: We have just completed our fire inspection of your office at 400 State Street in Springfield.[1] Unfortunately, there are several areas in which your company does not meet the minimum standards for[2] safety.

First, the wiring in the data processing center does not seem adequate to handle the large amount[3] of equipment you now have. We recommend, therefore, that you install a completely new wiring system in[4] order to prevent any possibility of electrical fire.

Second, there are too many desks in most of[5] your offices. In one case, there is a desk placed directly in front of the fire exit. This desk must be moved[6] immediately, and the total number of work stations should be reduced about 10 percent.

Third, we found no fire[7] extinguishers in the entire building. There is a city regulation that buildings must have at least one fire[8] extinguisher on each floor.

We know, Mr. Strong, that you will want to solve the problems immediately. We will[9] plan to visit your offices again within two or three weeks, and I am sure we will find things to be in much[10] better condition at that time. Yours truly,   [208]

7 Dear Ms. O'Donnell: Thank you for your letter of August 3. Most of the problems you found with our facilities[1] on your visit to our office have been corrected. We have rented an additional floor in the building and[2] have moved a number of our personnel to that floor. This solves the problem of having too many people in[3] several of the offices. There are now no exits blocked by desks; we comply with the city regulations concerning[4] such matters. In addition, we have placed fire extinguishers in various areas throughout the building.[5]

We do not feel that new wiring is necessary for the computer room. We have consulted James D. Owens,[6] one of the best electricians in Springfield, and he tells us that there is absolutely no electrical[7] hazard. He will be happy to supply you with any additional information you may need.

I hope you will[8] send one of your representatives back to our company as soon as possible to reassess our[9] facilities. Sincerely yours,   [184]

8 Dear Mr. Strong: You will be pleased to know that your offices are now in compliance with all the safety *standards*[*1] for the city of Springfield. We have checked each of the areas in which you received an unsatisfactory[2] rating during our first inspection, and each of the problems has been resolved.

After talking with an experienced[3] electrician, we have come to the conclusion that the wiring in your computer room is *adequate*[†] at[4] the present time. If you should add additional equipment, new wiring will definitely be required.

We will[5] check your building on an annual basis in the future as a part of our city's continuing efforts[6] to improve safety for everyone. Sincerely yours,   [130]
Also correct:
*regulations
†satisfactory

LESSON 49

4 Dear Depositor: The Commercial State Bank of Atlanta is happy to announce the plans for our new branch in[1] the Eastern Shopping Center. Our new building is being designed with you, our depositor, in mind. It will[2] feature all the regular banking facilities, which have always been available in our main branch at First and[3] Lee Streets. In addi-

tion, the new branch will introduce the latest innovations in the field of electronic[4] banking to residents of the area.

For the convenience of our depositors in the eastern part of[5] town, we will temporarily be operating in a frame building adjacent to our construction site. When[6] the new branch opens next September, you will be able to effect automated electronic funds transfer[7] simply by telephoning a special number at the bank.

If you desire to transfer your account to the new[8] branch, you may do so by stopping in at our temporary building and signing a short form. If you are unable[9] to come in yourself, you may call us at 555-3801 and we will complete the forms for you.

We[10] are working every day to make banking easier and more convenient for you. Sincerely yours, [217]

5 Dear Mr. Sweet: The management of the State Bank of Commerce is planning to introduce electronic check[1] processing to help speed up the work of the bank. Before we inaugurate our new program, however, we want to[2] be sure that all our employees are aware of all aspects of the changeover. We want to be sure that no one[3] feels that his or her job will be in jeopardy. We do not plan to discharge any of our present employees.[4] With the installation of our new equipment, we will actually be hiring several new employees.

We want[5] to make this changeover as easily and quickly as possible. The management of the bank feels that you are[6] the person who can best handle the human relations aspects of this job. If the program is explained fully[7] and completely, we believe all employees will readily accept it. Will you take on this responsibility,[8] Mr. Sweet? We sincerely hope that you will. However, should you decide that you yourself are unable to[9] accept this responsibility in addition to your regular work, perhaps you can recommend someone[10] else who could do the job.

Will you please stop in our office to discuss this matter at your convenience. Sincerely[11] yours, [221]

6 Dear Ms. McDonald: We are very glad that you have decided to install our new Model 200[1] electronic computer in your office at 110 West Main Street in Macon, Georgia. We will order the equipment[2] you need, and we should be able to do the installation sometime during the month of November.

Before the[3] actual installation, however, we must replace all wiring in your present computer room. We will plan[4] to begin the electrical work in your office in September so that we can connect the computer in[5] November. If you have any questions concerning our work, please feel free to call me any day between the hours[6] of 9 a.m. and 5 p.m.

We are happy to be able to work with you, Ms. McDonald, and we are sure[7] you will derive many benefits from your Model

200 computer. Yours truly, [156]

7 Dear Miss Henry: We are happy to send you a copy of our latest catalog, which describes all the new[1] electronic calculators we manufacture. We hope that you will be able to select a number of[2] calculators to sell in your retail store.

We have found that the Model 14 and the Model 18 are both very[3] good calculators. They can easily be converted from battery operation to standard electric[4] operation. They are both of excellent design and can be sold at a reasonable price and still[5] ensure you a good profit.

If you desire, we will send several of these calculators to you on a trial basis.[6] If they meet with general public approval, we hope you will decide to stock them on a regular basis.[7]

We are sure you will not be disappointed with our line of calculators, Miss Henry. Sincerely yours, [158]

8 Dear Miss Henry: We are very sorry that you do not *believe*[*] you would be able to market our calculators[1] profitably at your retail store in Phoenix, Arizona.

As you stated in your recent letter, we[2] do make calculators *basically*[†] for the commercial market. Unfortunately, we do not sell many[3] inexpensive calculators that could be retailed at a price below $50. However, our[4] subsidiary, the General Office Machine Manufacturing Company, does manufacture such calculators.[5]

If you desire to talk with them, please get in touch with Ms. Jane Carson, their sales representative, by[6] telephoning 555-9921. Sincerely yours, [130]
Also correct:
*think, feel
†primarily, principally

LESSON 50

3 *The New Industrial Revolution*
About 1850, America and the world experienced an[1] industrial revolution. Until that time, most goods were handmade. Artisans worked for hours or days on a[2] single product. But with the beginning of the industrial revolution, hundreds of items were mass - produced[3] by machines, which were relatively crude by today's standards.

Once mass production began, manufacturing took[4] gigantic leaps forward. Goods were available to hundreds of thousands of people who had formerly been[5] unable to acquire them. The rush from the farms and ranches to the cities began to swell the population of[6] the nation's great cities, and the United States changed from an agricultural society to an[7] industrial society.

With the invention of mechanical devices to manufacture goods, the[8] administrative work required to support this production also grew. Offices quickly sprang up near manufacturing[9] areas. Over the next 100 years the administrative employees sometimes outnumbered the[10] manufacturing personnel. A paperwork explosion rocked the nation. Offices were almost buried under[11] tons of paper. Government regulations added more and more paperwork to the already burdensome load.[12] The clerical work force grew quickly from 200,000 to 400,000. Soon there were more than 1 million[13] clerical employees, and the number continued to grow. Yet the paperwork continued to expand so[14] fast that the clerks simply could not keep up.

A way had to be found to process paperwork rapidly and[15] efficiently. Mechanical data processing became widely accepted in business about 1950.[16] Companies throughout the nation began to install mechanical data processing equipment.

Card punch machines,[17] sorters, and printers began to take over the tasks that had formerly been handled manually. After[18] information had been punched on cards, it could be sorted mechanically in a fraction of the time it had taken[19] to do it manually. Paragraphs and even complete pages could be printed in the time it formerly took[20] to type one or two words.

Computers were introduced into business in the next few years, and they were able to[21] perform quickly and efficiently functions that had ordinarily required days to complete. The new[22] industrial revolution had arrived.

By 1960 hundreds of banks, manufacturing companies, and[23] other institutions were making use of electronic computers.

Banks used computers to process checks. Many[24] organizations used computers to figure their payrolls. Companies used computers to handle all aspects[25] of tax computation. Computers seemed to be limited only by the imagination of those using[26] them.

However, an unexpected thing happened. The size of the work force did not drop drastically. The jobs that[27] clerks performed changed dramatically in character, but the number of employees continued to increase.[28] Instead of sorting papers by hand, employees were now operating electronic equipment. Instead of[29] making hundreds of mechanical computations, people were writing instructions that enabled computers to[30] perform the operations.

At first, most employees were afraid that the computer would take their jobs away. By[31] 1970, however, it was apparent that because business was now able to process many times[32] more work, employees were released to do other types of more advanced, challenging work.

Today the new industrial[33] revolution touches the lives of nearly everyone. Perhaps it is in the form of a bank statement that[34] is printed automatically. Perhaps it is the paycheck that is processed by computer. It may be a[35] class schedule in a public school or in a college that has been prepared by a computer. Few people feel[36] challenged by the computer today, and most look on this electronic marvel as a good friend.

It is difficult[37] to imagine what life would be like today or five or ten years from now without the aid of the computer.   [759]

CHAPTER 11

LESSON 51

3 Dear Mr. King: When you begin to plan your next vacation, let us have the privilege of helping you with all[1] the details. Our organization, the United States Travel and Transportation Company, has been in the[2] business of helping busy executives plan their business and pleasure trips for more than ten years.

We have on our staff[3] experts from every continent in the world. If you wish to plan a trip to the Orient, Mr. Smith, who lived[4] in China for many years, will help you with the details. If you would like to visit Europe, Ms. Chase, a former[5] resident of England, France, and Germany, will be happy to work with you. If you should want to visit Africa,[6] Miss Washington, who was born there, can be of great assistance to you. Each of these people and many others[7] on our staff can help you with everything from purchasing your airline tickets to arranging visits to[8] out-of-the-way places that tourists seldom see.

Just call us at 555-9923 for an appointment. There is,[9] of course, no fee for our services. Sincerely yours,   [190]

4 Dear Mr. Morris: Last week I was planning to travel on Smith Airline Flight 121 from Atlanta to[1] Birmingham. I had purchased my ticket several days ahead in order to be able to attend a meeting[2] of the National Manufacturing Association in Birmingham on August 21.

I had great[3] difficulty in getting to the air terminal because of the heavy traffic in the city. When I[4] arrived, I found that the plane was filled to capacity. I was told by the supervising agent that I would have[5] to wait for the next flight. I objected strenuously, but I was unable to convince the agent to[6] allow me to board the plane. As a result, I missed the first half of the meeting. Needless to say, this caused me great[7] anguish.

I understand there is a government regulation that protects travelers in such situations. Will[8] you please tell me exactly what I should do to assure myself that this type of incident will not happen[9] again. Yours truly,   [183]

5 Dear Mr. Swan: Thank you for your letter asking for information about governmental regulations of[1] airlines. We are glad to tell you about the rules that govern reservations.

On many flights there are a number[2] of people who make reservations and do not appear. In some cases people actually make two reservations[3] in order to be able to take an early flight if their schedule permits or a later flight if[4] necessary. This, of course, causes the airlines to have vacant seats that ordinarily could have been used by other[5] business executives or vacationers.

As a result, many airlines actually overbook their flights. In[6] a few isolated cases some passengers who have valid tickets are denied seats. If you arrive at least[7] ten minutes before the posted time of departure and are denied a seat, the airline has the responsibility[8] of getting you to your destination within two hours of your original expected arrival[9] time. If the airline cannot do so, you have a legitimate complaint against the airline. If you arrive less[10] than ten minutes before departure time, the airline has the right to cancel your reservation.

We suggest that[11] you take this matter up promptly with an officer of the airline involved. If we can be of further service[12] to you, Mr. Swan, please let us know. Sincerely yours,   [250]

6 Dear Dr. Murphy: I was particularly delighted to receive your letter in yesterday's mail; we[1] certainly can help to plan the type of tour to Europe that you wish to take.

My organization, The National[2] Travel Service, has a special department that plans trips for those who wish to see how people actually live in[3] various countries throughout the world. Miss Jane Yale, who heads this department, can arrange for you to stay in the homes of[4] residents of each of the countries you wish to visit. Of course, this means that you will see how the residents live[5] on a daily basis. Frankly, Dr. Murphy,

we feel that this type of trip is more valuable to both the[6] traveler and the hosts themselves than a regular vacation, which gives only a surface view of the actual[7] way of life.

I suggest that you call Miss Yale any weekday between the hours of nine in the morning and five in[8] the afternoon to make an appointment. She will be happy to set up a time that will be mutually convenient[9] to plan your interesting, educational vacation. Miss Yale's telephone number is 555-8102;[10] she will be looking forward to hearing from you. Sincerely yours,   [214]

7 Dear Mr. Poland: Last year I used your organization to help me and my family plan our annual[1] vacation. As you will probably remember, we visited a number of states in the East. I must say that[2] my family and I were very happy with the entire vacation, which we regarded as the best we[3] ever had taken.

We are now making plans for this year's vacation, and we would like your company to plan the trip[4] for us once again. At this time we are tentatively planning to visit three or four states in the West. We have[5] never been to the states of California, Washington, or Oregon, and we would like to see the usual sights.[6] We will wish to travel by air to California and then rent a car and drive to Washington. We want to spend[7] several weeks' time in the West during the months of June and July. We also want to spend at least part of the time[8] camping out in the mountains, but we would like to stay in hotels and motels during the remainder of the trip.[9]

Will you please let us know as soon as possible if you can help us with our plans. Sincerely yours, [197]

8 Dear Miss White: This summer I am planning to visit Europe, and I would like your company, The National[1] Travel Service, to help me plan my trip. I *ordinarily** like to take care of all the details of a vacation[2] myself, but I am very busy at this particular time and cannot make the arrangements.

In the past[3] I visited England, France, and Spain. This time, however, I wish to visit Italy and Germany. I do[4] not wish to have an ordinary tour of these countries; I want to spend at least a week's time in each country in[5] order to learn more about the people who live there. I do not want to stay in regular hotels; I *prefer*†[6] to stay in local inns that are frequented by the residents of the country. I do not wish to see the[7] usual tourist attractions; I prefer to see each of the countries from an insider's viewpoint.

Can you help me[8] with my plans, Miss White? If your company can arrange such a trip, I hope you will let me know as soon as[9] possible. I will be looking forward to hearing from you. Sincerely yours, [193]

Also correct:
**usually, generally
†want, wish

LESSON 52

5 Dear Mr. Garcia: Thank you for your letter of Thursday, February 3; we were very glad to hear from[1] you. I am sorry to have to tell you that we will not be able to accommodate your group at the Vermont[2] Hotel during your annual tour this spring. At this time we are renovating our entire hotel, and we will[3] not be able to open our doors again until next summer.

I would like to make a suggestion, however.[4] The Smith Hotel, which is located at 121 First Street, is open for business at this time and can[5] easily handle large groups. The Smith Hotel offers first-class accommodations with modern, up-to-date facilities,[6] and special group rates are available. If you wish to make reservations at the Smith Hotel, write to Miss[7] Janet Stern, who is the assistant manager there.

We hope, Mr. Garcia, that we will be able to serve[8] you ourselves next year. Sincerely yours, [167]

6 Ladies and Gentlemen: The European Railway Company is proud to announce a new service to the[1] public beginning Wednesday, March 21. On that date we will offer our new Explore Europe Tours. Exactly what[2] is an Explore Europe Tour? It is just what the name implies. It is a tour on which you can actually explore[3] almost every country in Europe. You can take tours of one, two, or three months.

For one basic price you get[4]

unlimited travel on any of our trains. All you need do is call at least one day ahead to make sure that a seat[5] will be reserved for you.

Now is the time for you to explore Europe. For further information, just fill out and[6] return the enclosed card. We will be happy to send you our complete folder. Sincerely yours, [137]

7 Dear Mrs. Edwards: I think you will be glad to hear about a new service that the Maryland Bank will begin[1] offering to many of its depositors in January. At that time we will offer to a select[2] group of our depositors our new check-guarantee card. The card will be available only to those who have[3] the very highest credit rating. We are glad to say that you are one of those people.

You may use the card in[4] any cooperating bank throughout the United States, and you will be able to cash a check for any[5] amount up to $500. Even if you are in Connecticut or California, you can cash a[6] check just as easily as you could here in Maryland. All you need do is present your card at any bank that[7] displays the check-guarantee symbol; your check will be cashed in a matter of seconds.

Just drop by our bank between[8] the hours of 9 a.m. and 3 p.m. any weekday, and we will issue your card. Sincerely yours, [178]

8 Dear Mr. Moore: It was a pleasure planning your recent vacation trip for you; we hope you found our services[1] to be satisfactory.

We are enclosing a questionnaire that I hope you will fill out and *return** to us[2] at your convenience. We would like to have your opinion of the service of the airlines, at the hotels, and at[3] the other places you visited. It will take only a few minutes' time to fill out the form, and it will help[4] us to serve you better in the future.

The next time you plan a *vacation*,† I hope you will let us have the[5] opportunity to serve you again. Very sincerely yours, [111]
Also correct:
*mail, send
†trip

LESSON 53

4 Dear Ms. Best: I just read in today's newspaper that you have been appointed an executive vice president[1] of the Foreman Travel Agency. I was delighted to read of your promotion, but I was not surprised.[2] Congratulations, Ms. Best, on this fine accomplishment.

All of us here at the Pennsylvania Hardware Company,[3] your former employer, send our very best wishes to you. When you left our organization last year to take[4] a position with the Foreman Travel Agency, we knew that it would not be long until you were promoted[5] to a position of major importance. Your new position represents a wonderful advancement for you.[6]

We know you are very busy, but please do not forget your old friends here at the hardware company. If you[7] happen to be in the area, we hope you will stop in for a few minutes and tell us all about your new job.[8] We are looking forward to seeing you again. Sincerely yours,   [172]

5 Dear Mr. Kennedy: Thank you very much for your letter congratulating me on my recent promotion.[1] I honestly appreciate your comments. I often think of you and the other members of your staff at the[2] Pennsylvania Hardware Company. My four years there gave me the background I need to handle a position of[3] greater responsibility. In my new position with the Foreman Travel Agency, I will be[4] responsible for both short-range and long-range planning.

In a few months' time I will be moving to the company's main[5] office at 410 Fourth Avenue, which is near your company. I will certainly accept your kind invitation[6] to visit you and tell you all about my new job. If you happen to be in the vicinity of my[7] present office, which is located on the second floor of the building at 140 State Street, please drop in to see[8] me. Sincerely yours, [164]

6 Dear Mr. Casey: As you will remember, last year the General Travel Agency had another record-setting[1] year. We made travel plans for more than 5,000 people throughout the East. Our gross income for the year was[2] more than $500,000, and our net profit represented an increase of more than 10 percent[3] over the previous year's. Needless to say, we are delighted with our record.

This was the fourth consecutive[4] year we have set new records, and the forecast for this year is very bright. If this forecast is correct, we should be[5] able to increase our business by as much as 10 percent. In order to do so, however, we must all put[6] forth an extra effort. Please express my earnest compliments to the members of your staff and encourage them to[7] do an even better job this year. Yours truly,
[149]

7 Dear Mr. Keith: We are very glad to announce to the public that General Airlines will begin operating[1] several new air routes from New York to cities in Africa. Beginning Tuesday, October 1, we are[2] opening our new direct service from New York to Cape Town. On October 12 we will inaugurate service to[3] the Gold Coast.

We are also happy to announce that we have just installed the latest, most up-to-date computer[4] hardware and software to help make our reservation service the fastest, most efficient in the world.

If you have[5] occasion to fly to Africa, just call us at 555-1701; one of our courteous[6] representatives will confirm your reservation immediately. We look forward to the privilege of[7] serving you. Sincerely yours,   [144]

8 Dear Ms. Kelly: The next time you plan to visit Asia, why not let one of our expert travel agents help you[1] with your arrange-

ments. We can make getting ready for your Asian vacation almost as much fun as the vacation[2] itself.

One of our representatives will be glad to help you plan every detail. In addition to the[3] regular services we provide, our well-trained staff can make valuable suggestions about interesting,[4] intriguing places to visit. They can also recommend the best places to eat in every country in Asia.[5]

We are enclosing a form that lists many of the countries in Asia. If you would like to have more information[6] about any of them, just place a check by the name of the country and return the form to us in the[7] envelope that is also enclosed. We will be glad to send you one of our beautiful four-color brochures for[8] every country checked. Sincerely yours, [167]

9 Dear Mr. Lopez: On Monday, January 5, the Eastern Travel Agency will open the doors of its[1] office at 8201 Fourth Street in the suburb of Boston, Massachusetts. We have rented two floors in[2] the Wilson Office Building, which is one of the most beautiful new buildings in the area.

Fourteen years[3] ago the Eastern Travel Agency opened its main office in the uptown section of Boston. We will, of course,[4] keep that office open. Beginning in January, *however,** you will have the choice of using either the[5] uptown or the suburban office.

The next time you need the *services*† of a travel agency, I hope you[6] will call on us. We are looking forward to hearing from you. Yours truly, [133]
Also correct:
*though
†help, assistance

LESSON 54

4 Dear Mrs. Gomez: If your travel agency is looking for good people, our organization can help you.[1] If your company is like most companies throughout the country, you have trouble finding just the right people for[2] the right positions.

Sometimes you may hire people who turn out to be poorly qualified, uninterested, or[3] even disloyal. Of course, this is a great disappointment to any company. It is quite difficult for[4] a company whose major business is not directly related to personnel work to find exactly the[5] right people for the right jobs.

This, Mrs. Gomez, is just where we can be of service to you. The International[6] Personnel Agency has had over ten years' experience in locating, testing, and placing people.[7] When an applicant comes to us, we find out all there is to know about his or her background, skills, and abilities.[8] When we place an employee with you, we guarantee satisfaction. If for any reason you are not[9] satisfied with the person, you simply notify us. The person returns to our office, and you pay us nothing.[10] On the other hand, if the person turns out to be the one you need for the job, you pay us only a small fee[11] based on the person's annual salary.

Isn't it in your own self-interest to take advantage of our[12] service? If you are interested in receiving further information about our organization, just[13] call us Monday through Friday between nine and four. Sincerely yours, [272]

5 To All Club Members: Once again this year the employees' organization of the Knoxville Manufacturing[1] Company is sponsoring its annual summer vacation tour.

On Friday, June 21, members of our[2] club will leave the main office here in Baltimore for a four-week tour of Norway, Sweden, and Denmark. We will[3] visit many world-famous historical sites en route. In addition, we will stay in some of the world's finest, most[4] unusual hotels.

For one special low fee we will furnish all transportation, lodging, and meals for the[5] entire trip. In addition, you will be admitted free to all major attractions.

The cost of the entire trip will[6] be only $2,000 double occupancy or $3,000 single occupancy. A[7] deposit of $100 will hold your reservation until May 15, when the balance will be due. Make[8] your reservation today; you will be making no mistake. Betty Smith, Vice President [176]

6 Dear Mr. Lexington: Your name was given to me by a mutual friend, Ms. Mary Brown. Ms. Brown tells me that[1] you will be graduated from Western College in a few months with a degree in French. She also tells me that[2] you are interested in working overseas as a travel guide for one or two years.

Our organization,[3] The World Travel Agency, employs people all over the world in positions as travel guides. At the present[4] time we have an opening for a person who can speak French fluently to serve as a travel guide in cities[5] throughout France. If you are interested in applying for this position, please let us know as soon as possible.[6] We will furnish you with all the necessary forms to make a formal application and arrange for a[7] personal interview.

We hope to hear from you soon. Cordially Yours, [153]

7 Dear Mr. Simms: If your travel agency has any employees who you feel are qualified for advancement[1] to your main office, we believe that we may have a service that will be of interest to you.

The International[2] Relocation Service can help your employees with the very difficult job of finding suitable homes[3] for themselves and their families when they are transferred from one city to another. We have highly trained professional[4] personnel in every major city in the world. These people can help your promising executives[5] on the way up to find houses in the type of neighborhoods in which they want to live. They can help them take the worry[6] out of investing a large amount of money in a house in an unfamiliar area.

All you need[7] do to take advantage of this service is furnish us with the names of your executives and the city to[8] which they will be moving; we will do the rest. Cordially yours,   [171]

8 Dear Miss Tate: Thank you for your invitation to take part in the annual convention of the National[1] Travel Association. I wish I could attend the meeting. Unfortunately, I am scheduled to be out of[2] the country at that time and will be unable to attend.

If it is *permissible,** I would like to send my[3] assistant, Miss Jane Klein, to represent me at the convention. Miss Klein has been on my staff for six months, and[4] attending a meeting such as this one would be a good experience for her.

Will you please let me know as soon as[5] possible if it is *satisfactory*† for Miss Klein to attend the convention in my place. Thank you for your[6] help; I look forward to hearing from you. Sincerely yours,   [130]
Also correct:
*possible
†all right

LESSON 55

3 *Exploring the World*
Statistics show that there are thousands of people living in the United States who haven't[1] seen any state other than their own. It is also a statistical fact that there are many people living[2] within a few hundred miles of the Atlantic or Pacific Oceans who haven't seen these great bodies of[3] water. People frequently get caught up in the events of everyday life and don't do the things that would make them[4] happier, better-educated persons.

Travel is one of the best ways to broaden one's outlook. It is, of course,[5] possible to read about the customs of people in distant states or in foreign countries, but there is no[6] substitute for actually seeing and meeting people in other parts of the world. Talking with people who live[7] very different lives from your own can help you to understand other people's attitudes and problems. It can[8] also help you to see their side of complex problems.

One of the first things you will notice about people when you[9] travel from one area to another is that people speak somewhat differently from region to region. A[10] difference of 100 or 200 miles can affect accent or pronunciation significantly. In[11] addition, words take on various shades of meaning from one locality to another. It may be a[12] little difficult for you to adjust to another person's speech, but after a few minutes' time, you will be[13] able to understand every word. Some people who are particularly good at hearing various sounds almost[14] immediately begin to imitate unconsciously the accent of those they are with.

Something you will notice[15] immediately when you travel is that people don't all eat the same kinds of foods. In some countries the foods[16] are bland; in other countries the people enjoy highly seasoned foods. It often surprises travelers to find out[17] that the foods they expect to find in a foreign country are not the usual diet.

In some countries people eat[18] meats and vegetables that are not considered edible in other lands. In some countries various types of[19] meats and vegetables that are considered staples in our country are left untouched. It may take a bit of[20] extra nerve to try a food that you have not eaten before, but the risk is usually worth it. Even if you don't[21] particularly like the food, you have gained a new experience. In addition, there is a chance that you will[22] enjoy the food immensely.

At the World's Fair, which was held in New York in the summer of 1965,[23] many people ate foods from foreign lands. They found these foods at special exhibits set up by each of the countries[24] represented. In a number of cases the foods were so well accepted by the people that permanent restaurants[25] were established in New York. These restaurants are thriving to this day. It wouldn't be unfair to say that the[26] World's Fair and the restaurants at the fair were directly responsible for a great deal of foreign travel.[27]

Something else that will catch your eye immediately when you travel away from home is that people dress differently[28] from area to area. Climate plays an important role in the way people dress, but custom and fashion[29] are equally important. Children in some countries all dress the same; in other countries you will notice great[30] variety. In some societies women's clothing is quite detailed and intricately made; in other[31] societies it is the men's clothing that receives the most attention. The work, the ideas, and the customs of the[32] people all influence clothing styles significantly.

When you travel to another state or country, however,[33] it is not the speech, the food, or the dress that should be of greatest interest to you. What should be of the most[34] interest are the people themselves. Even with basic language differences, people often find that they have more[35] in common with people in other lands than they believed. It is this kind of feeling that you bring home from a trip[36] that makes travel truly one of the best educational experiences you can have.

[737]

CHAPTER 12

LESSON 56

4 Dear Commuter: After more than seven years of service to the people of Chicago, the Jennings Bus Company[1] is going out of business.

As you probably know, our business has decreased substantially during the past[2] few years as a direct result of the new commuter trains that began serving the area. Although we have[3] a number of faithful, loyal patrons, we have been operating in the red for more than two years.

We had hoped[4] that we would

be able to obtain a government subsidy to help us continue operations at least[5] on a reduced basis. However, both city and state officials feel that this is unfeasible. We have no[6] choice, therefore, but to discontinue service.

We want to express our sincere thanks to all our riders who have been[7] loyal to our organization over the years and wish them the very best for the future. Sincerely yours,[8]   [160]

5 Dear Mr. Flynn: What is good public transportation worth to you? I think you will agree that it is worth a great[1] deal. It is virtually impossible for businesses to function properly in a large city such as ours[2] without a first-class public transportation system.

At the present time our public transportation system is[3] experiencing severe difficulty. Our business has decreased 5 percent during the past year, and our net[4] income has declined even more. If we do not have an increase in public support, we will soon be faced with the[5] possibility of a substantial curtailment of service. It may be necessary, in fact, to reduce[6] the number of trains and subways by as much as 10 percent.

We have only two possible alternatives at[7] this time. We can either increase the fares, or we can appeal directly to the state government for financial[8] assistance.

Will you please help us at this critical time by writing to your state government officials to let[9] them know just how valuable you personally feel public transportation is. Sincerely yours,   [197]

6 Ms. Smith: As you know, our company has experienced a great deal of trouble with the traffic congestion[1] at the main entrance to our building on First Avenue between Fourth and Fifth Streets. In order to alleviate[2] this problem, we are remodeling the entrance on Second Avenue. In addition, we plan to redecorate[3] and refurbish the interior of this entrance.

For the next three months, the Second Avenue entrance will[4] be closed in order to facilitate the remodeling. I hope you and the other members of your staff will[5] bear with us during this time. Mary Johnson   [108]

7 Dear Mr. Chang: General Airlines has just opened its new uptown office in the Smith Building at 412 East[1] Main Street in Detroit, Michigan. Because your company is located only a few blocks away from this[2] building, we believe that you will find our new office *particularly** convenient.

The next time you want to plan a[3] business trip, just drop by our new office. One of our representatives will be very glad to help you. We are[4] open from 8 a.m. until 5:30 p.m. Monday through Friday. In addition, we are open from 9[5]a.m. until 12 noon on Saturday.

If you find it inconvenient to

stop by our office, you can still[6] handle most of your travel *arrangements*[†] simply by dialing (800) 555-3102. Sincerely[7] yours, [141]

Also correct:

*very, extremely

[†]plans

LESSON 57

5 Dear Mrs. Trent: Thank you very much for the invitation to attend the regional transportation planning[1] seminar to be held on Tuesday, April 21, in Lexington, Kentucky. I sincerely wish that it[2] were possible for me to attend the conference. Unfortunately, I will not be able to be there[3] because I have accepted an invitation to attend a similar conference in Washington on that date.[4] If I can be of any help to you in planning your conference, I will be happy to do so.

If there[5] is any other way in which I can be of service to your organization, I hope you will let me know. You[6] can ordinarily reach me at my office between the hours of nine and five daily. Sincerely yours, [138]

6 Dear Miss Park: Mr. James Ford has applied for a position in the sales office of Huntington Bus Lines and has[1] supplied us with your name as a business and character reference. Mr. Ford tells us that he worked for[2] your manufacturing company for a period of three years as a sales correspondent before leaving to accept[3] a position as a sales representative with Brown and Company. Will

you please verify this information.[4]

In addition, we would like to know if Mr. Ford was a competent, dependable employee and if[5] he could plan and organize his own work successfully. If you will be good enough to give us this information,[6] Miss Park, you will have our gratitude. Cordially yours, [130]

7 Dear Mr. Cunningham: Thank you for your invitation to Mr. James Stern to give the keynote address at the[1] next regular meeting of the American Business Club. At this time Mr. Stern is away from the office[2] on an extended business trip, and he will not be back in the city until sometime late in May. Therefore, I[3] am afraid that he will not be able to accept your invitation.

Ms. May White, Mr. Stern's former[4] associate at Central Airlines, might be able to make a short presentation for your club. If you would like to get[5] in touch with Ms. White, you can reach her at 211 West 81 Street in Greenville, North Carolina. I[6] know Ms. White personally, and I am sure she will be able to do an excellent job for you. Sincerely[7] yours, [141]

8 Dear Dr. Case: As you requested several months ago, we sent you a special credit card to use at any[1] time you wanted to travel on Burlington Airlines. Our records show that as of today you have not used this card.[2] We had hoped, Dr. Case, that you would find the credit card an invaluable aid in planning your shopping, business,[3] and professional trips.

The Burlington credit card allows you to make reservations on any one of our[4] more than 100 daily flights to more than 50 cities throughout the United States. With the credit card all[5] you need do is call for your reservation, and when you arrive at the airport, one of our representatives[6] will insert your card into the computer terminal and your ticket will be charged automatically to[7] your account.

Won't you try out this new service the next time you plan a trip, Dr. Case? Sincerely yours, [158]

9 Ladies and Gentlemen: The town meeting that was held last Saturday morning in the high school auditorium[1] at 211 Washington Street in Huntington was an unqualified success. There were over 1,000[2] people in attendance, and more than 100 of them actually made short talks before the group. The topics ranged[3] from improving traffic flow in the uptown area to establishing a suburban community college.[4]

The city government now has a much better idea of exactly what the citizens wish to see done[5] during the coming year. Very truly yours, [108]

10 Dear Mr. Morris: Your letter asking for a recommendation for Mr. William Brown *arrived** in today's[1] mail. I am happy to give you the information I have about Mr. Brown's performance while he was on the[2] staff of the Ar-

kansas Transportation Company.

Mr. Brown began work here about six months ago. He did[3] acceptable work during the first few weeks. However, he was out of the office for more than a month because[4] of illness. When he *returned†* to work, his health did not permit him to work on a full-time basis. Therefore, he worked[5] only three or four hours a day. After six months he accepted a position with another company; my[6] records do not show the name of the new company.

I am sorry, Mr. Morris, that I cannot give further[7] information about Mr. Brown. Yours truly, [149]

Also correct:
*came
†came back

LESSON 58

4 Dear Mr. Higgins: For some time it has been apparent that the Central Bus Terminal is inadequate to[1] handle the ever-increasing number of commuters that pass through its portals daily. We realize that it is[2] not possible to add any space to our present location. Therefore, we have decided to relocate the[3] terminal in another section of the city.

We are presently looking at three sites. The first site is on[4] Main Street near the train terminal. The second site is on Elm Drive, where an old factory was located in the[5] past. The third site is fairly near the present location, but using it would require razing several buildings.

We[6] would like your opinion,

Mr. Higgins, as to which site would be best for the new bus terminal. Will you please[7] review the enclosed plans and let us know which of the possible locations you feel would be the best. Sincerely yours,[8]   [160]

5   Dear Miss Lee: Several days ago I received the preliminary plans for the new building at the air[1] terminal. I have reviewed the plans, and they look very good. However, I am afraid that there are several things[2] that should be modified if the plans are to be adopted.

First, the traffic flow around the building must be[3] simplified. There should be some accommodation made to separate buses, automobiles, and other surface[4] transportation.

Second, there should be some type of bridge connecting the old terminal building and the new one. I would[5] like to suggest that the two buildings be connected by an enclosed, climate-controlled concourse.

Third, the site of the[6] automobile parking building should be changed. I feel that the parking building should be located within easy[7] walking distance of both buildings.

Will you please consider these suggestions seriously and let me know your[8] final decision on each one of them. Sincerely yours,
[170]

6   Dear Ms. Chang: After more than two years' time, the new terminal building at the Denver Municipal Airport is[1] ready for op-

eration. On Wednesday, June 5, the building will be dedicated with a formal ribbon-cutting[2] ceremony, which will officially mark the grand opening of the terminal.

However, on Tuesday,[3] June 4, there will be a special preview showing of all the facilities in the building for local[4] officials and other dignitaries. We hope, Ms. Chang, that you will be able to join us for both events. The[5] preview will begin at 9 a.m. at the main entrance to the building. The formal opening will begin at noon[6] the following day.

Will you please take a few moments to fill out and return the enclosed self-addressed card to let[7] us know if you will be able to take part in these two activities. Cordially yours,   [156]

7   Miss Kennedy: Thank you for asking me to review the article on transportation that you wrote for the next[1] issue of our magazine. Congratulations on the fine job you did. The article shows that you have great[2] insight into the problems of mass transportation.

There are only a few things that I believe you should consider[3] modifying. I think it would be a good idea to verify the statistics on page 3 of the article.[4] Several of the numbers appear to be a bit too high. It might also be a good idea to simplify[5] the article in order to make it somewhat easier to read. I also think that you should make a little[6] better connection between the last paragraph on page 5 and the conclusion on page 6.

If you would like me[7] to review the article in its final form, I will be glad to do so. Robert Brown

[156]

8 Dear Commuter: On Monday, February 3, we will begin construction of the new entrance to the subway[1] on Main Street between First Avenue and Lexington Drive.

While we are in the process of construction, it will be[2] necessary for those who ordinarily use the Main Street entrance to the subway to use a new, temporary[3] entrance located on First Avenue. The new entrance will be clearly marked, and it will actually be[4] larger than the old entrance. Therefore, there should be no congestion.

We appreciate your patience and understanding,[5] and we hope that you will suffer no hardship. The Transportation Authority

[115]

9 Mr. Payne: You will be happy to know that we have been able to find a suitable building for our office[1] in Pittsburgh, Pennsylvania. Just yesterday I *located** a suite of offices that should serve our needs for a[2] period of at least three or four years.

The offices are located in the Eastern Transportation Terminal[3] at 400 Lexington Drive. The offices were formerly occupied by the Smith Oil Company, which[4] vacated the premises only last week.

When you have an *opportunity,†* I hope you will stop by

the[5] building and let me know if you concur with me that we should sign a long-term lease immediately. Grace Washington[6]

[120]

Also correct:
*found
†chance

LESSON 59

4 Dear Mr. Lane: We were very much disturbed to receive your letter of Thursday, July 6, in which you wrote to us[1] about the incident in the automotive section of the American Department Store. It is our[2] policy, of course, to give our customers the best-quality goods at the lowest possible prices. In addition,[3] we always try to provide courteous, prompt, and efficient service.

The items you purchased in our store were[4] to have been delivered directly to you at your home in Wilmington. Unfortunately, they were misplaced in[5] our shipping room and never delivered.

When you reported this problem to the sales representative, Mr.[6] Alvin Yale, he should have located the package and sent it directly to you by messenger. We are very[7] sorry that you feel that Mr. Yale was discourteous to you. I discussed the matter with him, and he assured[8] me that he would not knowingly be rude to a customer. He felt that the problem was simply the result of[9] a misunderstanding.

Nevertheless, we want to apologize sincerely to you for any discourtesy[10] you experienced in our store. Your package should have reached you by now, Mr. Lane, and I hope you will give us[11] another chance soon to show you that we can provide prompt, courteous service. Sincerely yours, [237]

5 Dear Mr. Smith: Your letter of inquiry about the commuter train service in Philadelphia has been[1] referred to me. Thank you for expressing your concern about the reduction in the number of trains on the line[2] that serves your area.

We want you to know that we are not willingly reducing our service; it is a[3] matter of economic necessity. We also want to assure you that we will not reduce service during[4] the rush hours between seven and nine in the morning and between four and six in the evening. We are reducing[5] the number of trains during the other hours of the day. We hope that this reduction in service will be[6] temporary and that we will soon have full service restored on all lines.

We know that commuters have a choice of driving[7] to work, riding a bus, or taking a train. We definitely want you to choose our company, and we will do[8] everything in our power to be sure that our service is prompt and dependable. Sincerely yours, [178]

6 Dear Mr. Brothers: This is to acknowledge your letter in which you wrote about the poor service you have had on[1] our commuter rail line during the months of November, December, and January.

We realize, of course, that[2] our train service has not been up to our usual high standards during this time. However, we feel there is a[3] rational explanation.

As you know, the East is experiencing the worst winter in the past decade. On[4] three occasions we have had more than 12 inches of snow within a few hours' time. When this happens, our service[5] suffers.

Our employees have willingly worked many hours overtime this winter in the harsh weather. We have had to[6] cancel only four trains in November and five in December. Thus far, we have not had to cancel a single[7] train in January. While our trains are definitely running behind schedule, we are rather proud of the job[8] we have been doing under the trying circumstances.

I hope you will understand the problems we have had and[9] that you will continue to choose our commuter line as your principal means of transportation. Sincerely yours,[10] [200]

7 Dear Ms. Brown: I realize that your commuter rail company must receive many letters of complaint every day.[1] Public transportation companies have to contend with bad weather, employee strikes, and various other[2] problems every year. Many times companies are blamed for conditions over which they have little control. I want you[3] to know, Ms. Brown, that this letter is not one of censure; it is one of commendation.

On Thursday, February[4] 3, my

mother, who is quite elderly, was accompanying me on a train trip to Boston. We had been[5] riding on your train for about two hours when the train lost all power. It was nearly three hours before another[6] train came to pick up the passengers. During those three hours your employees did everything in their power to make[7] us comfortable. Even though the weather was bad and the outside temperature was below freezing, we were[8] not uncomfortable. Mr. Lee Garcia, one of your employees, willingly took off his coat to give to[9] my mother.

You may be sure that whenever I have a choice of transportation companies, I will definitely[10] choose yours. Sincerely yours, [205]

8 Dear Mr. Martin: Several weeks ago I ordered a copy of your latest publication, *Trains of History*.[1] I chose this particular book because of my great interest in trains.

In today's mail I *received** a copy[2] of *Yesterday's Trains*, a book that your company published more than two years ago. Evidently, there must be some[3] misunderstanding. I added this particular book to my *library†* last year, and, of course, I do not need[4] a second copy. I am, therefore, returning the book to you separately.

I would still like to receive a[5] copy of the new book. Sincerely yours, [107]

Also correct:
*got
†collection

3 *Our Shrinking World*

Since the Wright Brothers' first flight on that historic day in North Carolina, our world has been[1] shrinking almost every minute. No, it is not actually getting smaller, but it certainly seems that way. Before[2] the invention of the airplane, most people never ventured more than several hundred miles away from their homes. Of[3] course, automobiles and trains could run across a continent, but intercontinental travel took days or[4] even weeks before the invention of the airplane.

That first flight did not set many records by modern standards; it[5] was actually measured in terms of feet. Jetliners today have a wingspan greater than the length of the first[6] flight. When the Wright Brothers flew that short distance, however, they expanded geographic boundaries for countless[7] millions of people throughout the world.

Though the United States covers four time zones and is nearly 3,000 miles[8] across, jets can fly across the country in only five or six hours. In the early part of this century, the[9] great distance between the Atlantic and Pacific Oceans made it practically impossible for the[10] average person to see both the East and West Coasts. Now it is not[11] uncommon for a young person to have visited 15 or 20 states before graduating from high school. Some fortunate youngsters have actually visited[12] every state in the Union. Such travel would most certainly be impossible without the airplane.[13]

Supersonic jets can now travel across the Atlantic Ocean from the United States to Europe in only three[14] or four hours' time. It is possible to take a plane in London before sunrise, travel west across the[15] Atlantic to New York, and arrive before the sun catches up with you. This, of course, suddenly adds several hours to[16] the length of the day. This time will be lost on the return flight when the plane travels east.

It has not been too long since[17] people stopped to gaze at the sleek jetliners as they flew swiftly across the sky. Today it is uncommon to[18] see anyone even look up when a plane flies over. What was considered a miracle only a few years[19] ago has become commonplace.

One airline pilot from New York regularly buys French bread for his family.[20] Yes, it is actually made in Paris. Visitors to Hawaii often bring beautiful, freshly cut flowers[21] to their homes in the North in the middle of winter. It is not uncommon today for people who live in one[22] state to go to another state on a shopping excursion.

Sometimes a number of air companies cover the[23] same routes. This occurs in areas where there are many people who use the same route regularly. The airlines[24] compete vigorously for the right to serve the traveling public in these areas. In general, both[25] increases and decreases in fares are regulated by the federal government. Therefore, the airlines must[26] attract passengers with other types of incentives. Some airlines offer stereo music; others offer motion[27] picture entertainment in flight. Some offer special food service. It has become the amenities that have won[28] many riders over from one airline to another. If you were to ask what most people want from air service,[29] however, they would say that they want fast, efficient, and safe planes. In addition, they want courteous, friendly flight[30] attendants.

Air travel has made our world seem smaller by making remote areas easily accessible.[31] Air travel has brought people together from all over the world. The airplane touches the lives of everyone.   [639]

CHAPTER 13

LESSON 61

Office-Style Dictation
2 (*As dictated*) Dear Mr. Tate: Our company will be opening a new branch in Moline on Monday, January 5. At the present time we have possible openings (*take out possible*) for three or four new employees. We need an office manager and two or three secretaries. If you know of any employees (make that *people*) you feel would be excellent (no, *good*) employees, I hope you will let us know as soon as possible. (Take out *as soon as possible*.) We would like to interview them as soon as possible.

You may be sure, Mr. Tate, that we will be glad to return the favor if we can be of service to you in the future. Very sincerely yours,

2 (*As it would be transcribed*) Dear Mr. Tate: Our company will be opening a new branch in Moline on Monday, January 5. At[1] the present time we have openings for three or four new employees. We need an office manager and two[2] or three secretaries. If you know of any people you feel would be good employees, I hope you will let us know.[3] We would like to interview them as soon as possible.

You may be sure, Mr. Tate, that we will be glad to[4] return the favor if we can be of service to you in the future. Very sincerely yours, [97]

4 Dear Miss Short: It is indeed a pleasure to welcome you as a new member of the public relations department[1] of the Worth Advertising Company. You come to us with an excellent record in the field of public[2] relations, and we are sure that you will add much to the effectiveness of our organization.

When you come[3] to work on January 15, please report directly to the personnel department, where you will take part[4] in an orientation program designed to acquaint you with the various aspects of our business.

If you[5] have any questions concerning the Worth Advertising Company, please feel free to call me any morning[6] between the hours of 9 a.m. and 12 noon. Sin-

cerely yours, [130]

5 Dear Mr. Grant: I was particularly glad to see that you have hired Mr. Sam Davis to head the[1] public relations department of our organization. I have known Sam for many years, and I have great confidence[2] in his ability to manage a large public relations department such as ours.

I know you will find[3] Sam to be a person of good character and personal integrity. In addition, you will find that he[4] will be very well accepted by all those who work with him and for him.

When Sam arrives in town, I hope you will[5] let me know; I would like to take him to lunch or dinner during his first week with our organization. Sincerely[6] yours, [121]

6 Dear Mrs. Bennington: I am happy to write a letter of recommendation for Mr. Carl O'Brien,[1] who worked for my organization several years ago. During his tenure with us, Mr. O'Brien established[2] himself as one of the brightest, most dependable members of my staff. It was with a great deal of reluctance[3] that I accepted his resignation last year when he decided to move to another part of the[4] country.

I am sure, Mrs. Bennington, that you will be making no mistake by hiring Mr. O'Brien. If you[5] have any questions about his ability, I hope you will feel free to call me. Sincerely yours, [118]

7 Dear Miss Brown: This is to acknowledge your request for information about one of our for-

mer employees, Miss[1] Helen Yale. Miss Yale worked in my department several years ago. However, that was before I became head of[2] the department. I have looked into Miss Yale's personnel record, and apparently she was on the staff for[3] only a short period of time. In fact, there are only two or three persons here who remember her, and only[4] one of them feels confident to give a personal recommendation.

I am sorry that I cannot be of[5] more help to you, Miss Brown. Perhaps you will be able to get more information from Miss Yale's last employer. Sincerely[6] yours, [121]

8 Dear Mr. Moore: We are looking for a good person to head the new public relations department that we are[1] adding to our *organization** sometime after the first of the year. If you know of anyone who would do[2] a good job for us, I hope you will let us know as soon as possible.

The person we need should have at least three[3] years' experience in the field of public relations. In addition, we want a dependable person who[4] can work well with people. We are planning a public relations department of at least ten people. These employees[5] will all report directly to the new *manager.*†

We will appreciate any help that you can give us[6] in locating the right person for the job, Mr. Moore. Sincerely yours, [133]
Also correct:
*company, business
†person

5 Mr. Harris: I was glad to hear that you have been able to locate a person to fill the position that[1] you had open in your public relations department. Ms. Mary Cunningham, the person you hired, seems to[2] have just the qualifications you need.

I am sorry that I was not able to work with you personally[3] in selecting someone to head this department. As you know, I have been in Birmingham, Alabama, on business[4] for the past several weeks. I am sure, however, that you have selected the best candidate for the job.

When[5] Ms. Cunningham reports to work, please ask her to come to the personnel department to fill out the necessary[6] forms for our files. May Hardy [126]

6 Dear Mr. Sample: Do people recognize your company's name when they hear it? Does the name of your organization[1] automatically make people think of a company noted for its efficiency and[2] dependability? When your representatives call on prospective clients, are the clients glad to see them? If you[3] cannot answer yes to these questions, your company does not have a good public image.

My organization,[4] the Framingham Public Relations Company, specializes in helping companies create a new, positive[5] public image. We can handle all aspects of public relations work; we can plan a total public[6] relations program for you. We have created public relations programs for hundreds of companies throughout the[7] nation. Many of them have increased their business by as much as 20 percent simply because of our work.

Why[8] not let one of our local representatives come to see you soon and explain exactly what we can do for[9] you. You will be under no obligation, of course. Sincerely yours, [193]

7 Dear Miss Blain: Several years ago the General Retail Company was a small organization with only[1] one store in Centerville, Iowa. Today the General Retail Company has a local store in Centerville[2] and also operates in major cities in Idaho, Missouri, and Wisconsin. By the end of the[3] year the General Retail Company will be operating in more than ten states.

What caused this phenomenal[4] growth? Good business practices, of course, had a great deal to do with it. However, General hired our[5] organization, National Public Relations Associates, to help get their message across to the buying[6] public. In only a few years' time we have been able to give the General Retail Company an entirely[7] new image. We have helped them to increase their annual sales from $200,000 to more than[8] $2 million.

We can do the same thing for your company, Miss Blain. If you will call us at 555-1601,[9] our local representative will be glad to visit you and discuss all our services. Sincerely[10] yours, [201]

8 Miss King: Enclosed is a copy of the advertising brochure that was prepared for us by the Middle States[1] Advertising Company. As you will recall, we wanted to use the brochure to help create a new image for[2] our company.

I am sure that the brochure actually will create a new image for us; however, the[3] image will probably be very bad. I think that the work is substandard. It appears to have been written in a[4] hurry and printed carelessly.

Will you please let me know what you think about this, Miss King. Frank Stern [97]

9 Mr. Stern: I have just *finished** reading the advertising brochure that was prepared for us by the Middle States[1] Advertising Company. I must agree with you, Mr. Stern, that the work is substandard. I am afraid that[2] we will not be able to use the brochure in our current advertising campaign.

Because the Middle States[3] Advertising Company has given us such *poor*† service for the past month, I think we should cancel our[4] contract immediately. Will you please take whatever steps are necessary to effect this cancellation. Ruth[5] King [101]
Also correct:
*completed
†bad

LESSON 63

4 Dear Sir or Madam: If the letterhead paper you use is not of top quality, you may be damaging your[1] business. This may seem

to be an unusual thing to say, but it is important to remember that[2] a company's letterhead may carry as much impact as its sales force.

Some business executives may feel that a good[3] way to decrease costs is to buy cheaper paper. However, this kind of thinking usually hurts business. If the[4] public image of a company is cheapened because of poor-quality paper, little has been gained. In fact,[5] business may actually be lost.

Be a wise executive; examine your company's letterhead today. If[6] it makes a poor impression on you, chances are that it will do just the same with those who receive your correspondence.[7]

Let one of our experienced representatives design a beautiful letterhead on high-quality[8] paper for your company. Just fill out and return the enclosed postage-paid card; we will call you within a few[9] days. Sincerely yours, [184]

5 Dear Mr. Keith: Would you say it is fair to judge a company by the quality of its letterhead paper?[1] Some business executives would say no. However, many executives actually do judge a company[2] by the quality of its stationery.

Johnson Business Forms Company specializes in providing[3] top-quality stationery to business firms throughout the United States. We can supply you with the type of[4] stationery products you will be proud to use. In addition, we can supply these products to you at a price that[5] is more than fair.

To receive a sample packet of our fine papers, just fill out and return the enclosed postal[6] card. Sincerely yours, [124]

6 Dear Miss Quinn: The members of the Chamber of Commerce of Springfield are delighted that you are considering our[1] city as the site for next year's convention of the Home Building Association. I would like to take a[2] moment to tell you about some of the wonderful advantages that our city has to offer a group such as[3] yours.

We have an abundant supply of high-quality hotel rooms within easy walking distance of the[4] fairgrounds, where the convention facilities are located. We have some of the world's finest restaurants located[5] throughout the city. In addition, we have a safe, efficient public transportation system that charges[6] very low fares.

I think you will be pleased with the unusually high quality of all the types of services that[7] we can offer your group. I hope you will accept our invitation to spend a weekend with us sometime in the[8] near future to let us show you just what we have to offer. Cordially yours, [174]

7 Dear Mr. Green: Several weeks ago I ordered a one-year supply of stationery products to be used by[1] the members of my office staff. I ordered 100 reams of executive letterhead paper, 12 gross of[2] pencils, 20 boxes of envelopes, and various other supplies.

The total price for all of these

items[3] as shown in your catalog was $2,000, which I considered to be fair. Several days after I sent[4] my order to you, I received a note from your representative stating that the prices had to be increased[5] and that the bill would exceed the original estimate by 3 percent. This was satisfactory with me,[6] and I asked that your company go ahead and process the order.

Last week the order arrived at the local[7] post office; today the bill came. It was nearly 25 percent higher than the original estimate.[8] Evidently, someone else's purchases have been posted to my account.

Will you please check your records and send[9] me a correct bill. I will process payment just as soon as I receive a correct statement. Yours truly,   [198]

8 Dear Miss Short: Thank you very much for your letter asking for information about employment in the[1] manufacturing department of the Brown Publishing Company. We are always very glad to hear from college students[2] who are interested in pursuing a career in the publishing field. I am happy to answer your[3] specific questions about our employment practices.

We are an affirmative-action, equal-opportunity[4] employer. Any person with knowledge, skill, and perseverance will have no difficulty in obtaining[5] employment with our company or in advancing after initial employment.

When we have an opening[6] in any division, we usually advertise it in several editions of the newspapers throughout[7] the states of Mississippi, Alabama, and Georgia. We actually have 20 or 30 applicants for[8] every position we have open.

After the initial screening, we ask 10 or 11 of the applicants[9] to come in for a personal interview. Each of the applicants is interviewed by at least three people,[10] and the best person for the job is eventually selected.

If you have any further questions about our[11] employment practices, Miss Short, I hope you will feel free to call me. My telephone number is 555-8102.[12] Very truly yours,   [246]

9 Dear Ms. Lee: It was a *genuine** pleasure meeting you when you visited Springfield, Oklahoma, last weekend.[1] I think you will agree with me that our city would be the *ideal*† place for your convention next year.

We are sending[2] each of the members of your committee a standing invitation to visit our city as our guests[3] anytime before the convention. We sincerely hope that you will recommend Springfield as the site for your convention.[4]

If there is anything we can do to help you in making your final decision, please do not hesitate[5] to let us know. We are looking forward to hearing from you, Ms. Lee. Very cordially yours,   [117]
Also correct:
*real
†best

LESSON 64

4 Dear Miss Keith: During the spring semester I will be teaching a course in public relations at Huntington[1] College here in Wisconsin. I would like to have one of your representatives come to speak at one class session.

The[2] class will meet from 5 to 7 p.m. on Tuesday and Thursday evenings beginning February 25.[3] I anticipate that there will be at least 30 members in the class; all of them will be graduate students[4] working on advanced degrees in business administration. Some of them will be full-time students, but many of[5] them will be part-time students who work in businesses on a regular basis.

I would like someone from your[6] company to present a general lecture on the nature of work in a large public relations firm. If you[7] think it will be possible for one of your employees to come to speak to our class, please call me at[8] 555-7102. I will be looking forward to hearing from you. Yours very truly, [176]

5 Dear Mr. Hayden: About four years ago I became interested in the field of public relations, and[1] I enrolled in an undergraduate program in Huntington College in Wisconsin. In June I will be[2] graduated, and I would like very much to work for a well-known public relations firm such as yours.

Although I[3] have had no actual experience working in the field, I have taken part in the work-experience[4] program sponsored by the college. I worked part time in the public relations department of the Smith Furniture Company.[5] Mrs. Shirley James, head of the public relations department there, has given me permission to use[6] her name as a reference. I am enclosing a personal data sheet that gives a complete record of my[7] educational background.

If it is not inconvenient for you, I would like to come to your office for a[8] personal interview during the week of June 5. I hope to be working for your company in the near[9] future; I believe I can make a significant contribution to your organization. Sincerely yours, [199]

6 Dear Ms. White: Thank you very much for your fine presentation at the annual meeting of the American[1] Public Relations Association. The audience found your informal manner appealing and your subject[2] stimulating. We had many comments about how much the participants got from your talk, Ms. White. Congratulations[3] on a job well done.

I hope that you will be available to make a similar presentation to[4] our organization at next year's meeting. I will be getting in touch with you before the program is planned.[5] Very truly yours, [103]

7 Dear Mrs. Smith: As you probably know, the city of Springfield is making an all-out attempt to attract the[1] national convention of the Home Building Association next year. This convention annually draws more than[2] 30,000 people to the host city, and it would be very good for the economy of the entire[3] state if the association decided to meet here next year.

We are asking business executives throughout[4] the city to write to each of the members of the convention site committee to try to persuade them to choose[5] Springfield for the convention. I hope you will send a letter to one or more of the members listed on the[6] attached sheet. If you write to them, emphasize the availability of a large number of hotel rooms in the[7] immediate area, the excellent restaurants in the vicinity, and the low transportation fares.[8]

Please let me know if you will cooperate with us in this venture. Sincerely yours, [175]

8 Dear Ms. Lopez: We are happy to report that the auditors have completed their work on your company's books[1] for last year and that they found them to be in good shape. There were only one or two minor inconsistencies that[2] your accountant will be able to correct very easily.

We would like to bring the records to your office[3] and discuss these problems with you personally on Thursday, January 14, at ten in the morning. If[4] this time is inconvenient for you, please call us and we will select another time. Very sincerely yours, [99]

9 Dear Mr. Tarkington: Several weeks ago I applied for a position with your public relations[1] company. As yet I have not had a response, and I am wondering if you have selected another applicant.[2]

If you have not yet filled the position and are still considering my application, I hope you will let[3] me know. I am quite naturally interested in working for a well-known company such as yours.

I hope you will[4] give me the opportunity, Mr. Tarkington, to show you what I can do for your company. You can reach[5] me between the hours of nine and five at 555-9208. Sincerely yours, [115]

10 Dear Mr. White: On a recent business trip I met a member of your accounting staff, Ms. Jane Davis. I asked[1] Ms. Davis about possible employment in the public relations department of your organization,[2] and she suggested that I write to you.

In the near future I will be moving to New York, and I am definitely[3] interested in working for your company. I have a degree in business administration from Harper[4] State College. My work experience includes three years in the personnel department of Jennings Industries[5] in Detroit and two years in the public relations department of International Industries in Memphis.[6]

Enclosed is a complete personal data sheet. May I have an interview with you, Mr. White? I will look forward[7] to hearing from you soon. Sincerely yours, [148]

11 Ladies and Gentlemen: Have your profits been going up during recent years? Have you been able to increase your[1] sales by as much as 5 percent or 10 percent during each of the past three years? If you cannot answer yes to[2] these questions, perhaps the failure has been caused by poor public relations. If this is the *case,** perhaps I can be[3] of help to you.

My organization, the Southern Public Relations Company, has helped businesses such as[4] yours for more than ten years, and we should be able to help you too. The Southern Public Relations Company can[5] help you formulate a complete program of public relations.

We usually begin with an informal[6] survey to determine *exactly†* what the public thinks about your company. We then design a special program[7] for you that we believe will be of great benefit in improving your company's public image.

If you would[8] like to have one of our experienced, well-trained representatives call on you, just drop us a line at[9] 436 Main Street here in Columbus, Ohio. We hope to hear from you in the near future. Sincerely yours,   [199]
Also correct:
*problem
†just

LESSON 65

3 *Public Relations*
Some companies work for years to build up business but somehow never manage to achieve their[1] ultimate goals. They may have spent large sums of money on development. They may have invested vast amounts on[2] equipment and supplies. They may have even spent a great amount of money on recruitment and training. But[3] somehow the money they invested in the company never actually paid off. Why is this true? Perhaps the[4] reason is that the company lacked good public relations.

Public relations involves the way the general[5] public perceives a business. A company may be relatively small, but the public may think of it as a large,[6] impersonal organization. Another may be a large multinational company, but the public[7] may think of it as a small, family-owned business. The way the public perceives a company is largely a[8] matter of public relations.

Large companies often put a large percentage of their advertising budget[9] into the area of general public relations. They do this to get the public to think of the[10] company as a warm, personal organization rather than a large, cold business. It is in a company's[11] best interest to invest in this kind of publicity.

There are a number of ways that a large business[12] invests money to show the public that it is a genuine member of the community. The company may[13] support civic activities on a local level. For example, a large company may become an active[14] financial supporter of local hospitals, libraries, or various other nonprofit organizations.[15] The company may encourage its employees to join the local United Fund to help support worthwhile[16] community projects. Or the company may give substantial grants or scholarships to a local college or[17] university. All of these things can help the large company seem smaller and less distant to the average[18] person.

Businesses can improve public relations in ways other than subsidization of local projects. Management[19] may encourage employees to join local civic clubs and to take a part in neighborhood activities.[20] The people of the community begin to feel closer to a company that had formerly seemed very[21] distant.

Sometimes companies give their busy executives a chance to take off a few hours a week for a[22] period of a year or so to work with a group of Boy Scouts or Girl Scouts or to chair a committee of the[23] Chamber of Commerce. The company may even ask one of its executives to serve as the financial consultant[24] to a civic organization.

These things help the local organization, and they also help the[25] employees to feel that they are a real part of the community. The result is that a company improves its[26] image and its profits at the same time by investing time and money in the sensitive area of[27] public relations.   [543]

4 *A Career in Public Relations*

Public relations is a field that attracts many people because it seems glamorous and interesting. It[1] can be an extremely interesting field, of course, but it is one that requires talent and patience as well[2] as education and experience.

The person who wants to work in public relations will find that a college[3] background is usually a necessity. This is because most companies want their public relations[4] personnel to be knowledgeable in the areas of advertising, marketing, and psychology. In[5] addition, they want their employees to be experts in the field of human relations. In short, a person who[6] works in public relations often has to have a great deal of knowledge in many areas, and a good[7] college is probably the best place to acquire this knowledge.

It is true, of course, that any employee of a[8] business actually represents his or her company to the general public. But it is particularly[9] true in the field of public relations. Actions of individuals are quite likely to be[10] interpreted as actions of the company. It is, therefore, extremely important that the public relations[11] employee always act in a way that will not bring discredit to the company. The public relations employee[12] should do everything possible to enhance the reputation of the company. Whether or not the[13] action taken by the employee is directly related to company business, the employee has the[14] opportunity to help the company improve its image.

The public relations specialist will find himself[15] or herself working in a constantly changing field. The specialist may work in various industries and[16] locations. However, one thing will never change. The public relations specialist must always work with people. There[17] will be people within the department, of course. There will also be many people who work for the company[18] outside the department. And there will be the public in general.

The public relations specialist must[19] always deal with people with genuine respect and courtesy. The theories learned in college will be of great help, of[20] course. However, there is no substitute for experience.

A career in public relations can be[21] interesting and rewarding, but it requires much patience and common sense.   [434]

CHAPTER 14
LESSON 66

Office-Style Dictation
2 *(As dictated)* Dear Ms. Gray: We were, of course, very glad to receive your letter of October 23. (Make that *Monday, October 23.*) Thank you for your order. We will send it after (no, *immediately after*) we run a routine credit check. We must do this, of course, for all new customers. However, this should take no more than a week's time, and you will soon have the books you need for your spring classes. (That should be *fall classes.*)

I am enclosing a copy of our new catalog (add the word *fall* before *catalog*). In it you will find a number of books you may wish to buy (change that to *add*) to your library. Please send your order for any of these books. Yours truly,

2 *(As it would be transcribed)* Dear Ms. Gray: We were, of course, very glad to receive your letter of Monday, October 23. Thank you for[1] your order. We will send it immediately after we run a routine credit check. We must do this, of course,[2] for all new customers. However, this should take no more than a week's time, and you will soon have the books you need for[3] your fall classes.

I am enclosing a copy of our new fall catalog. In it you will find a number of[4] books you may wish to add to your library. Please send your order for any of these books. Yours truly,   [98]

4 Dear Ms. Wayne: We are delighted to announce that the Pennsylvania Publishing Association will have[1] Dr. Mildred Johnson as the principal speaker at its annual meeting in Harrisburg on February[2] 3, 4, and 5. We know that every member of our organization will want to be at the meeting to hear[3] Dr. Johnson.

Unfortunately, we have not been able to find a hotel with a meeting room large enough[4] to accommodate all the people we expect. Therefore, we have asked Dr. Johnson to give her talk twice, and she[5] has graciously consented to do so. She will speak on the subject of setting and meeting goals at 9 a.m.[6] on February 3 and again at 9 a.m. on February 4. Both her presentations will be made[7] in the Gold Room of the Hotel Baker at 405 Main Street in Harrisburg.

Don't be left out; make your[8] reservation for this very important conference now. You may do so by filling out and returning the enclosed[9] card. Sincerely yours, [184]

5 Dear Dr. Short: The General Publishing Association will hold its annual convention this year on[1] Friday and Saturday, August 3 and 4. The meeting will be in the main conference room at the Hotel President[2] at 275 State Street in Chicago, Illinois. I hope you will make your plans now to attend.

The[3] featured speaker at this year's meeting will be Dr. Paul Wood, who holds a position of great responsibility[4] with the state government in Illinois. He will talk on the subject of government regulations in the[5] publishing industry. I am sure that this subject will be of particular interest to everyone in[6] attendance.

To make your reservation, just fill out the enclosed form and mail it to us with a check for[7] $65. This will cover your registration fee and one night at the hotel. We look forward to seeing you[8] in Chicago. Sincerely yours, [166]

6 Dear Ms. Wilson: Thank you for your letter asking for information about Mr. Kenneth Cunningham, one of[1] my former employees. Your letter arrived in this morning's mail. I am very glad to serve as a business and[2] character reference for Mr. Cunningham.

Mr. Cunningham began working for my company as a[3] correspondence clerk ten years ago. He did his work efficiently and satisfactorily and never[4] refused to accept difficult assignments. In only one year Mr. Cunningham was promoted to a position[5] of greater importance in the publications division of the company. He quickly established[6] himself as a person of dependability, perseverance, and integrity. He progressed rapidly, and[7] within 2 years he became manager of the division.

Mr. Cunningham's experience in the[8] publications division laid the groundwork for his eventual promotion to director of advertising for[9] the company. He served in this position until he resigned last year to return to college to complete his[10] master's degree.

I am very glad to be able to give Mr. Cunningham a good recommendation. If[11] we had a position open on our staff at this time, I would definitely ask him to return to our[12] company. Very truly yours, [245]

7 Dear Dr. Temple: Thank you very much for the suggestions you *mailed** to us on ways to improve our new college[1] accounting text; we appreciate your sharing your ideas with us.

Mrs. Betty Smith, who is managing[2] director of the accounting department, is away from the office on an extended business trip. When she[3] *returns,†* I will see that she gets a complete copy of your suggestions.

I am taking this opportunity to[4] send you a copy of our new catalog. When you have an opportunity, I hope you will look through it and[5] place an order for any texts you will be needing for your classes next fall.

Best wishes to you, Dr. Temple,[6] for an interesting, successful school year. Sincerely yours, [131]

Also correct:
*sent
†comes back

LESSON 67

5 Dear Dr. James: Thank you very much for sending me a copy of your recent publication, *Fundamentals[1] of Management*, for review. I think it is one of the best books of its kind available today. You have done[2] a fine job in making a rather difficult subject both easy and interesting. I do not know of[3] any other book on the market in the field of management that is so well written and so easy to understand.[4]

Congratulations, Dr. James, on the excellent job you have done. You may be sure that I will recommend[5] your text whenever the occasion arises. Yours truly, [111]

6 Dear Miss Carson: The faculty of the language department here at West High School in Reno, Nevada, is[1] interested in a new, innovative way of teaching foreign languages to our students. We understand that your[2] company has just published a new learning system that is designed to teach Spanish and French on an individual[3] basis.

If you have not done a research study using the new materials, we hope you will let us[4] conduct the project for you. We would like very much to do this during the coming school year. We have done this type of[5] experiment frequently in the past, and the results are usually very good.

If you could let us have three[6] or four copies of the student learning materials, we would be happy to conduct a carefully controlled[7] study and give you the results free of charge.

Will you please let us hear from you soon. Sincerely yours, [157]

7 Dear Mr. Drake: Thank you very much for sending me an examination copy of the new text, *The Self-Reliant[1] Person*. The authors have done an excellent job in presenting a great deal of information in a[2] logical, systematic, and interesting way. They have used a new approach that is entirely different from[3] any other I have seen. I have read the book carefully, and I have decided that I would like to use it[4] in my human relations class during the spring semester.

Because the spring term is only three weeks away, I[5] will need to have the books delivered immediately. Will you please send 20 copies of the text to the Smith[6] College bookstore at 201 Elm Drive in Vicksburg, Mississippi. You may include a bill with the order, and[7] the manager of the bookstore, Ms. Mary White, will send you a check immediately.

I am looking forward[8] to using your new text in my class beginning next month. Yours truly, [173]

8 Dear Mrs. Kelly: We are happy to announce the publication of a new book in the field of international[1] marketing. It was written by one of the most respected authors in the United States, Dr. Lee[2] Gordon. The new text, *International Marketing Today*, is now available for delivery in time[3] for your fall classes.

As you know, Dr. Gordon is an assistant professor of marketing at Brown College[4] in West Virginia. During the past three years Dr. Gordon has been compiling statistics to include in his[5] new book. He has done an excellent job, and this publication is the most timely, up-to-date text available[6] today.

If you do not have a text for your fall class in international marketing, I hope you will[7] consider adopting this new book. Let us send you a free examination copy; just fill out, sign, and return[8] the enclosed card today. Sincerely yours, [167]

9 Dear Ms. Jones: For the past three years it has been a pleasure for us to serve your school by supplying many of the[1] textbooks you need for your *classes.** However, in the past six months you have not placed a single order for new books[2] from our company, and we are wondering what the *problem†* could be.

If our products do not meet your needs, we would[3] like to know where they fail. If one of our sales representatives has not done something you wished, we want to know[4] about it. If you have just not needed any new

books during the past six months, we would also like to know that.

Please[5] take a moment's time to jot down the reason on the back of this letter and return it to us in the enclosed[6] envelope. We hope that you will let us have the opportunity to continue to serve you, Ms. Jones. Sincerely[7] yours, [141]

Also correct:
*students
†trouble

LESSON 68

4 Dear Miss Ball: We are happy to send you a copy of our new textbook, *Cooperative Education*. When you[1] receive the book, will you please take a few minutes to examine it carefully. We especially want to call[2] your attention to Part 1, which includes chapters on American free enterprise and the role of education[3] in business today.

We would also like you to notice the thought-provoking questions at the end of each[4] chapter. Note particularly the interesting questions after Chapter 12, "Getting Along With Your Associates."[5] In addition, please take special note of the carefully selected case studies at the end of each unit.[6]

We believe, Miss Ball, that you will agree with us that *Cooperative Education* is the best, most up-to-date[7] textbook available in its field. If you decide to use *Cooperative Education* in your classes this[8] fall, just call your local representative, Mrs. Alice Smith; she will be glad to accept your order. Sincerely[9] yours, [181]

5 Dear Professor Paul: Thank you for sending the new material for your book, *Consumer Education;* you have[1] done a splendid job. I am happy to tell you that we are on schedule with the production of your book; we[2] expect to have copies available by the end of January. This will give us an ample amount of time[3] to get the books into the teachers' hands before the start of the fall term.

We are now designing the workbook to[4] accompany the text. I am making several minor changes in the format. I do not believe we have left[5] enough room after each question for the students to write answers. Therefore, I am adding two extra lines after[6] each of the questions. In addition, I am leaving extra room after each case study for the students to write[7] in their comments.

These changes will not require any work on your part. They will, however, make the workbook[8] 24 pages longer. If all goes well, the workbook should be available shortly after the textbook is published.[9] Sincerely yours, [183]

6 Dear Mr. Small: As you know, the field of consumer education is a growing one, and there is a demand[1] for a good new textbook. For the past several years, I have been working on a manuscript for such a textbook.

The[2] manuscript contains 400 double-spaced typewritten pages; it should provide enough material for a[3] textbook of about 200 pages. In addition, I have pre-

pared a student workbook and a handbook for[4] the instructor. I am sure that these materials can be produced with very little editing.

If you would[5] like me to send you a copy of my manuscript, please call me any weekday at my office. I am there[6] between the hours of 9 a.m. and 5 p.m. Sincerely yours, [131]

7 Dear Mr. Ford: If you are considering remodeling your home in the near future, I am sure you will be[1] interested in the new book that our company has just published. The title of this interesting, informative[2] book is *Remodeling Your House.*

The book gives in concise, easy-to-read language many helpful suggestions[3] on just how to remodel every room in your house. There is a chapter on effective ways to remodel[4] your living room and dining room. There is a chapter on how to convert an extra bedroom into a den or[5] a playroom. In addition, there is a complete chapter on how to install new plumbing in your bathroom and[6] kitchen.

If you would like to have a copy of this new book, just fill out and return the enclosed card today. You need[7] send no money at this time; we will bill you later. Take a minute or two now to order your copy of[8] *Remodeling Your House;* you will be glad you did. Yours truly, [170]

8 Dear Dr. Mendez: We are happy to announce publication of our new college textbook, *Modern*

Insurance,[1] by Dr. Paul Brown, professor of business at Eastern State College in Newburgh. Dr. Brown's new book is the best,[2] most up-to-date text in its field available for college classes today. It contains chapters on life, health, and[3] accident insurance. In addition, it contains a separate chapter on coinsurance.

If you would like[4] to *receive** a free examination copy of *Modern Insurance,* all you need do is *call*† Mr. Alvin[5] Carpenter, our local representative in your area. His telephone number is 555-2101.[6] Cordially yours, [124]
Also correct:
*get, have
†phone, contact

LESSON 69

4 Dear Mrs. Swanson: I have just completed a manuscript for a new book in the field of office efficiency.[1] It has taken me several years to finish it, and I feel that it will probably be a very good[2] seller on the college market.

As you know, I usually work with the Franklin and Myers Publishing Company.[3] However, that company has another book on office efficiency on the market now, and the management[4] there feels that it would be a mistake to publish a similar book at this time. I am, therefore, looking for[5] another publisher. Do you know of another company that is looking for a good manuscript in this[6] field? If you do, I would be happy to send the company a copy of the foreword and several chapters of[7] the manuscript for review.

Thank you for your help, Mrs. Swanson; I look forward to hearing from you soon. Sincerely[8] yours, [161]

5 Dear Mr. Washington: You will be happy to know that your new book, *Reliable Transportation Systems,* is[1] now being typeset. If all goes well, we should have copies off press within three or four months.

At this time there are[2] several things that we would like you to do. First, we would like you to write a foreword for the book. Second, if you plan[3] to have an acknowledgment page, please furnish us with the appropriate copy. Third, please supply us with a signed[4] release from each of the people you used as models in the photographs in the book.

We are sure that your new book[5] on transportation will be a very good seller, Mr. Washington. We will look forward to receiving a[6] letter from you by return mail. Sincerely yours, [129]

6 Ladies and Gentlemen: Three months ago I canceled my subscription to your magazine, *Transportation Times.* I[1] had been a regular subscriber for more than four years. I looked forward each month to receiving the magazine,[2] which I considered to be one of the best on the market.

During the past year, however, I had trouble[3] getting the magazine. Several times it came more than a month late. On three occasions I did not receive the magazine[4] at all. Finally, I decided it would be easier for me to purchase a copy of the magazine[5] each month at the local bookstore. Therefore, I canceled my subscription.

The magazine stopped coming; unfortunately,[6] the bills did not. For the past three months I have received bills for the magazine. Will you please look into this[7] matter as soon as possible and see that I do not receive any further bills. Yours truly,   [157]

7 Dear Miss Wood: I have just finished reading your latest book, *Fashion Design for the Beginner.* I want to congratulate[1] you on the fine job you have done on this book, Miss Wood. In my opinion, it is by far the best book of[2] its type available today. From the foreword to the last page, one can easily see the special care you took[3] to make this book sensible, practical, and informative.

I have purchased several copies of the book to use[4] as gifts for my friends. I know that each of them will find the book to be just as helpful as I have. I am looking[5] forward to reading your next book. Sincerely yours,   [109]

8 Dear Mrs. Morris: Thank you very much for sending us a copy of the manuscript for your new textbook,[1] *Transcribing Practices and Procedures.* The book is certainly well written, and you have done a thorough, careful job.[2] I wish sincerely, Mrs. Morris, that it were possible for us to publish this book for you. However, we[3] are already in the process of typesetting a similar book, *Advanced Transcription,* and we

cannot publish[4] another.

I am sure you can easily understand why we must reject your manuscript. If you have other[5] ideas for books, we would certainly be happy to hear about them.

We are returning your manuscript[6] separately.   Sincerely yours,   [124]

9 Dear Dr. Smith: Our new college textbook, *Business Communications,* is now available for fall *adoption.**[1] We think that once you have had an opportunity to review the book, you will agree with us that it is one[2] of the best books available in its field.

The first part contains a section on letters of goodwill. The second[3] part is devoted to letters of credit and collection. The *remaining*† parts cover the various other[4] areas of business communication.

Let us send you a free examination copy of *Business[5] Communications.* It will, of course, place you under no obligation to adopt the text for your classes. Yours[6] very truly,   [122]
Also correct:
*classes, use
†other

LESSON 70

3 *A Job as a Newspaper Reporter*
Many stories have been written about the field of newspaper reporting.[1] In addition, a great many of these stories have been turned into dramas for both the cinema and[2] television. People are usually interested in stories

dealing with the preparation and publication[3] of news.

A myth has grown up around newspaper publishing. The jobs of the men and women who work in a[4] newspaper office are supposed to be romantic and glamorous. In actuality, however, most of[5] the jobs are neither romantic nor glamorous. They are demanding, tedious jobs that require long hours of[6] careful work.

An editor for a newspaper may put in many more hours a day than he or she actually gets[7] paid for. An editor working on a particularly large project may begin work at 6 a.m. or[8] 7 a.m. and work until 8 p.m. or even later. People who work such long hours often do so to[9] establish their reputation or to get ahead in the field.

Many college graduates who have majored in the[10] field of journalism apply for positions with local newspapers only to find out that the work they do[11] is quite different from their preconceived ideas. They may be asked to take over a seemingly unimportant[12] job while more experienced writers cover the major stories. This can be very discouraging to new employees,[13] but as with any other field of endeavor, promotion and advancement depend on how well the young employees[14] do the easy, routine jobs. The young reporters who can handle small jobs in an efficient, dependable[15] manner will find themselves in line for a promotion.

Just as in other fields, newspaper publishers often hire[16] employees at fairly low starting salaries, which can also be discouraging to the beginning[17] reporter. However, those employees who do exceptional work will soon get ahead and quickly move away from[18] the employees whose work is only marginal.

Within a short time both the level of work and the[19] remuneration will increase for the above-average employee. An exceptional reporter is often promoted[20] within a few months' time, and most employees who do worthwhile work receive a promotion within a year.

A[21] newspaper reporter must be able to make a routine story seem interesting and important. Of course, facts[22] cannot be manipulated, but they can be presented in ways that invite the reader to go ahead and[23] finish reading the entire story. The reporter must strive to obtain the reader's attention with an[24] interesting opening paragraph. Sensationalism, of course, is not what the writer wants. Rather, a human[25] interest or intriguing opening is the goal.

In the remaining paragraphs of the story, all the[26] pertinent facts must be presented in a logical, orderly manner that gives the reader every bit of[27] information needed in a relatively small amount of space.

The job of the reporter in the newspaper[28] field is a very good one, but it is one that does not have the glamour ordinarily associated[29] with it. It requires many hours of hard work combined with logical thinking and good writing skills. For the person[30] who wants to be a newspaper writer, however, the field offers interesting, challenging work. [618]

4 *Publishing a Book*

The next time you are in a public library or a bookstore, take a close look at any one of the books on[1] the shelves. As you look through the pages, think of the many men and women who were involved in putting the book[2] together. Most people are not aware of how much time and effort go into the publication of a single[3] book.

There are many people actively involved in the publishing process. There is, of course, the author. His or[4] her name will ordinarily appear directly under the title on the front cover of the book. However,[5] there are many other people who make worthwhile contributions whose names may never appear anywhere in[6] the book. These people perform many specialized tasks. There are highly trained editors who evaluate the[7] original manuscript. When they have judged the manuscript to be acceptable, they turn it over to the[8] marketing staff. These people estimate how many copies are likely to be sold. Then the members of the production[9] staff determine just how much it would cost to print the book. The costs include the work of the designer, the[10] typesetter, and the printer. It may be that even though the book would make a worthwhile contribution to a specific[11] field, it is not feasible to go ahead with publication because the costs would exceed the expected[12] revenue.

If the costs are within reason and the sales estimates are large enough, the company will probably[13] go ahead with publication. When the finished product is placed on the shelf, it represents perhaps thousands[14] of hours of difficult, tedious work on the part of many people. [294]

CHAPTER 15

LESSON 71

Office-Style Dictation

2 *(As dictated)* Dear Mr. Smith: The report that you submitted is satisfactory (make that *good;* no, leave it *satisfactory*). However, I believe that you should make two or three basic changes in the report:

1. The opening section should be at least three (no, *two;* no, *three* is correct) pages in length.

2. The end of each section should include a short summary of the material in that particular section.

3. There should be a section on conclusions and recommendations added to the end of the report.

I want to thank you, Mr. Smith, for the work you have done on getting the report together in such a short period of time. I know that you and the members of your committee had a great deal of work to do and had to spend many hours of overtime in order to accomplish it.

When you have made these three basic changes, I am sure that the report will be exactly (change that to *just;* oh, I guess *exactly* is better) what we want. Sincerely yours,

2 *(As it would be transcribed)* Dear Mr. Smith: The report that you submitted is satisfactory. However, I believe that you should make[1] two or three basic changes in the report:

1. The opening section should be at least three pages in length.

2[2]. The end of each section should include a short summary of the material in that particular section.[3]

3. There should be a section on conclusions and recommendations added to the end of the report.

I want[4] to thank you, Mr. Smith, for the work you have done on getting the report together in such a short period[5] of time. I know that you and the members of your committee had a great deal of work to do and had to spend[6] many hours of overtime in order to accomplish it.

When you have made these three basic changes, I am sure that[7] the report will be exactly what we want. Sincerely yours, [152]

4 Ladies and Gentlemen: If you are not getting the most from your advertising budget, perhaps you should[1] investigate what our organization can offer you. My company, Yates Advertising Associates, has been[2] in the business of creating effective, productive advertising for clients for more than ten years. We have[3] a team of 25 experienced men and women who can handle every detail of your advertising[4] program. We can take your ideas and quickly turn them into an effective advertising campaign.

If you would[5] like to see just what we can do for you, please call Mr. Paul Patterson, our new-account executive. He will[6] be glad to spend several hours with you to tell you all about the wide range of services we offer. Sincerely[7] yours, [141]

5 Dear Mrs. Smith: A former employee of yours, Mr. James Washington, has applied for a position as a[1] correspondence clerk with the state government here in New Mexico. He has given us your name as a reference,[2] and we hope you will answer a few questions for us.

Will you please fill out the enclosed form telling us when[3] Mr. Washington began working for your advertising agency, how long he worked for you, and why he left. We[4] would also like to have any general information you may have about Mr. Washington's character,[5] ability, and initiative.

The job for which Mr. Washington is an applicant is a very[6] important one that requires security clearance. You will have our gratitude if you will give us a complete[7] reference. Sincerely yours, [144]

6 Dear Ms. Cunningham: I

would like to take this opportunity to thank you for the wonderful job your agency[1] did in developing the advertising campaign for our company several months ago. I am happy[2] to tell you that as a direct result of the advertising, our sales have increased by more than 15 percent,[3] which is a remarkable record for such a short period of time.

We have made a survey to determine[4] which part of the campaign had the greatest effect on our sales. The radio announcements had no particular[5] effect, but the television advertisements were of major importance. Unfortunately, the advertising[6] circulars, which we distributed throughout the entire area, seemed to be ineffective. The half-page[7] advertisement that was placed in the newspapers on three consecutive Sundays had a very great impact.

At[8] the present time we are planning to run another advertising campaign sometime next spring. Will you please begin[9] thinking about the type of advertising you believe would be most effective for us. We definitely[10] want the Cunningham Advertising Agency to plan the campaign for us. Very sincerely yours, [218]

7 Dear Mr. Moore: Advertising can make the difference between success and failure in business. Are you getting the[1] most from every advertising dollar that you spend? If you do not feel that your advertising budget is[2] being spent to obtain *satisfactory** results, it would be a very good idea for you to let us examine[3] your entire advertising program.

My organization, the Jennings Advertising Company, is new[4] in this area, and we have many new, exciting ideas about how we can help businesses such as yours[5] *increase*† sales. We have a staff of well-trained, responsible people who can quickly determine whether or not your[6] advertising budget is being invested properly.

If you would like to have one of our representatives[7] come to your office to speak with you, just call us at 555-1796. You will be making no[8] mistake by calling us, Mr. Moore. We will look forward to hearing from you. Sincerely yours, [176]
Also correct:
*good, the best
†improve

LESSON 72

5 Mr. Jones: Thank you very much for sending me a copy of the advertising circular for a new line[1] of women's and children's clothing. I want to congratulate the designer and the artist; they have both done[2] very good work. I am sure that our client will get many sales in the next few weeks as a direct result of this[3] fine circular.

There are, however, one or two things that I believe you should take note of before you publish your[4] next circular. Although the circular is very beautiful, I do not believe that you can justify[5] using a four-color format. Two colors would have about the same impact on sales with much less expense. By[6] eliminating two colors, I believe you could afford an eight-page circular instead of a four-page circular.[7]

If you will send me a copy of your preliminary design for your next circular two or three weeks[8] before you plan to have it published, I will be glad to evaluate it for you. Jane Lee [176]

6 Dear Miss Agronski: Thank you for your inquiry about the services our advertising company makes[1] available to organizations such as yours. We are very glad to tell you about the type of work we do.[2]

Our company offers a full range of advertising services. We have a well-trained staff of experienced,[3] professional people who know everything there is to know about every aspect of the advertising[4] business. We can plan radio, television, and newspaper advertising, which should increase your sales by as much[5] as 10 percent within only a few weeks' time.

In order for you to see just what we can do, you should spend a few[6] hours at our offices reviewing one of our successful advertising campaigns. Our office is located[7] at 402 14th Street in Detroit, Michigan. Will you please call me or one of our representatives at[8] 555-1682 to arrange for an appointment. We will select a date and time that will be all right[9] for both of us. We are looking forward to hearing from you. Sincerely yours, [194]

7 Dear Dr. Moore: It was a pleasure meeting you in Auburn, Alabama, on my recent business trip. I am[1] happy that you have decided to use the services of our advertising company during the coming[2] year.

I have asked several members of my staff to begin work on preliminary plans for your program of[3] advertising. They tell me that because of the size of the job, it will take at least three months to get the project[4] organized.

If it is all right with you, Dr. Moore, I will bring the plans to you sometime during the first week in[5] November. If you feel that you cannot wait until that time, please let me know. Sincerely yours, [116]

8 Dear Miss Edwards: You will remember that last year you conducted an advertising campaign for my company[1] to introduce a new line of women's shoes. My company, the Brownsville Shoe Store, was very well pleased with the work[2] that you did.

We actually increased sales more than 10 percent in the three months following the campaign. However, our[3] sales have fallen off recently, which leads us to believe that we should conduct a continuing advertising[4] campaign to keep our company name before the public.

Would you be interested in entering into a[5] long-term contract with my organization to prepare advertising? If you think you can do this, please let me know[6] as soon as possible; I will be looking forward to hearing from you.

Very sincerely yours, [137]

9 Dear Miss Brown: Some people feel that advertising is an expense. While this may be true in one sense, it is definitely[1] not true in another.

You do actually have to spend money on advertising, but the money that[2] you spend is usually very well invested. If you choose the right type of advertising, every cent that you[3] put into it pays off in added dollars to your income.

We can help you make the best use of every cent that[4] you spend for this purpose. Why not let one of our experienced representatives come to your offices to[5] explain our entire program to you. We hope to hear from you soon. Sincerely yours, [114]

10 Dear Mr. Jefferson: Thank you for the estimate you submitted for the advertising campaign that my[1] company wishes to conduct in the states of Michigan, Nebraska, and Minnesota. I was *pleased** with the type[2] of campaign you planned, but I was quite surprised at the estimated cost of $3,000. Frankly, I had[3] not planned to spend more than $1,000 for the entire project.

At this time I am faced with the problem of[4] deciding just what to do. I can limit the campaign to the state of Nebraska, or I can plan a less[5] comprehensive campaign to cover all three states.

When I have an *opportunity*† to evaluate the[6] situation thoroughly, I will get in touch with you again. Yours very truly, [134]

Also correct:
*happy, delighted
†chance

LESSON 73

4 Dear Mr. Best: My organization, the Hall Advertising Company, is planning to remodel its[1] office at 402 Sixth Avenue in Minneapolis, Minnesota, and we would like your construction[2] company to submit a bid for the work.

We plan to modernize our reception area and make six or[3] more small accounting offices where we now have two very large management offices. We also plan to[4] install new carpeting and lighting.

Will you please have someone from your company come to our office to analyze[5] our needs and advise us on just how much it would cost for you to do this work. We hope to hear from you soon. Yours[6] truly, [121]

5 Dear Ms. Smith: This is just a short note to thank you for the work you did in helping General Enterprises launch[1] our new line of office equipment last month. As you know, the advertising campaign, which was the largest our[2] company has ever attempted, was extremely successful. We are very happy with the results.

In two or[3] three months we will have had sufficient time to analyze all results, and we will be able to determine just[4] how much of the increase in our sales can be attributed to your advertising. We will very likely be[5] getting in touch with you to plan more advertising in the future. Sincerely yours, [115]

6 Dear Mr. Kelley: If you want to be sure that every dollar you spend on advertising is money well[1] invested, insist that all your advertising be placed with International Enterprises. Our organization[2] has the finest, most comprehensive advertising department in the East, and we can plan an effective,[3] money-making advertising campaign for you.

What is more, International Enterprises is large enough[4] to handle all your advertising and promotion on a continuing, long-term basis. You can count on us[5] to analyze your needs, plan your advertising, and execute the plan with a minimum investment on your[6] part. Isn't it in your own self-interest to insist that International handle all your advertising[7] in the future? Don't wait; call us today. Our telephone number is 555-8020. Very sincerely[8] yours, [161]

7 Dear Mr. Carter: Our accounting firm wishes to plan a series of advertisements to be used in the[1] area newspapers beginning February 21. We believe that we can increase our business substantially[2] if we let the general public know exactly what we can do for them. We realize, of course, that[3] accounting firms such as ours do not ordinarily advertise in newspapers. However, we believe that the[4] time has come for us to do so.

Will you please ask one of your account representatives to come to our office[5] sometime between the hours of 9 a.m. and 5 p.m. on January 3 to discuss the matter further.[6] Sincerely yours, [123]

8 Dear Ms. Moore: It is with a great deal of pleasure that I invite you to join the select group of people who are[1] members of the Western Advertising Association. By becoming a member, you will join a group of[2] forward-thinking business executives.

Membership in our organization gives you the opportunity[3] to exchange ideas with professional advertising managers from throughout the area. You will be able[4] to gain from their knowledge as they will gain from yours. You will be able to keep up with the latest ideas in[5] the field of advertising.

If you would like to have more information about the Western Advertising[6] Association, please fill out, sign, and return the enclosed card as soon as possible. Cordially yours, [138]

9 Dear Miss Moore: It was a pleasure *meeting** you last week when you came to my office to finalize your advertising[1] plans for next year. I would like to summarize briefly the things we decided to do.

First, we will begin work[2] immediately on the advertising campaign for the new line of women's and children's clothing that you plan[3] to introduce to the public on January 23.

Second, we will begin radio and[4] television advertising on either January 16 or 17. Please let us know which date you believe[5] would be better.

We are very glad to be able to assist you with the project, Miss Moore. We will get in touch with[6] you immediately whenever we have any ideas that we *believe*† will help you to merchandise your[7] products. Sincerely yours, [144]

Also correct:
*talking with, seeing, to meet
†think, feel

LESSON 74

4 Dear Ms. Keith: Mr. Alvin Cain has applied for a position on the faculty of the James School of[1] Advertising and has given you as a reference. Will you be good enough to supply me with answers to the[2] questions that are listed on the enclosed form? If you will do this, I will be extremely grateful.

I would like to know[3] if you think that Mr. Cain would be a good faculty member for us. Do you think he can inspire and motivate[4] the students? Can he assume a great deal of responsibility and work without a great deal of direct[5] supervision? Is he a person of integrity and dependability? In short, will he have a[6] positive overall effect on our school?

If you give Mr. Cain a good recommendation, I will give serious[7] consideration to adding him to the staff of the James School of Advertising. Sincerely yours, [158]

5 Dear Mr. Smith: If your regular advertising company is not getting the effect you want from the[1] money you invest, why not let the Jennings Advertising Agency handle your account. When you deal with us, you[2] will enjoy the benefits of working with one of the largest, best-known agencies in the West.

The Jennings[3] Advertising Agency can handle any type of advertising with sensibility and reliability.[4] We can give you standard advertising, or we can devise a unique program characterized by[5] novelty and ingenuity. You will never realize how much we can affect your company's income unless[6] you give us a try. To find out exactly what Jennings can do to increase the sales of your company, just fill[7] out and return the enclosed self-addressed card. You will not be disappointed, Mr. Smith. Sincerely yours, [158]

6 Dear Miss Stein: In just a few months' time I will be graduating from Page College with an advanced degree in[1] advertising. I am very much interested in working for a large, innovative advertising agency,[2] and I would like to apply for a position with your company.

Enclosed is a copy of my personal[3] data sheet, which describes my background and experience. I am also sending several letters of reference[4] from my former employers.

I truly believe, Miss Stein, that I can help you to effect a real increase in your[5] income. I hope you will give me an opportunity to come to your office for a personal interview.[6] May I hear from you soon. Sincerely yours, [127]

yours, [62]

7 Ladies and Gentlemen: We are pleased to enclose with this letter a copy of the annual financial[1] report of the Lexington Advertising Company. Will you please take a few minutes to look over the report[2] now. I think you will agree with the board of directors of our company that this is by far the most[3] encouraging financial report that we have published during the past ten years.

As you will remember, last year we were[4] somewhat disappointed with the return on investment. However, this year we have made a remarkable[5] recovery, and we have been able to effect an increase in both our gross income and our net profit.

Please note[6] especially the report on the acquisition of the Eastern Advertising Agency, a small company[7] located in Bangor, Maine. A full description of the agency is given on page 4. The effect of[8] this acquisition has been an increase of almost 10 percent in our net income.

We are justly proud of our[9] accomplishments this year, and we hope you will be too. Max Davis, President [194]

8 Dear Mr. Lopez: Thank you for your inquiry about the effect of new government regulations on the[1] advertising industry. I am enclosing a copy of a circular we published recently on the[2] subject.

If you have any specific questions, I encourage you to call your local representative.[3] Sincerely

9 Dear Mrs. Sloan: I am happy to tell you that we have selected you from more than 25 applicants for[1] the job of advertising writer for our company. The results of your writing examination were[2] superior, and we were very much impressed with your ability to answer difficult questions in a[3] logical, sensible way.

Will you please come to our medical department sometime before March 21 for a[4] complete physical examination. If the results of this examination are satisfactory, we[5] hope you will plan to *begin** work on Monday, April 2. As we *stated†* at the time of your interview, your[6] starting salary will be $18,000 per year. Sincerely yours, [134]
Also correct:
*start
†said, indicated

LESSON 75

3 *Advertising—A Window for Business*

If you were to ask people their opinion of advertising, many[1] of them would probably say that advertising adds to the price of goods. Some would estimate that advertising[2] adds perhaps $100 or more to the price of a television set. They might guess that advertising[3] would increase the price of a new automobile by $1,000 or even $2,000. In a[4] survey of over 1 million people a number of years ago, more than 50 percent stated that they felt[5] that advertising was not necessary and that it actually increased the cost of most consumer items.[6] Nothing could be further from the truth. The fact is that advertising actually decreases the cost of most goods[7] and services.

Consider for a moment what would happen if all advertising ceased. How would you know that a[8] new product had been introduced on the market? How would you know when a significant improvement had been made[9] in an existing product? How would you know when there was an abundant supply of a commodity, which could[10] bring the average unit cost down? The only way that most people would know about these things is by word of mouth, and[11] word of mouth travels very slowly and reaches only a few people.

The result would be that only a few[12] people would know when a new product was available. Only a few people would be aware that a[13] significant improvement had been made in an existing product. And only a few would know that there was an[14] oversupply of a certain commodity. Therefore, sales would not increase, and prices might increase.

Now let us suppose[15] that a newspaper ad for a new motor oil was placed in the Sunday, Monday, and Tuesday editions of just[16] one newspaper in a large city. The number of persons who would know about the new motor oil would increase[17] rapidly. Perhaps as many as 5,000 or 10,000 people would become aware of the new oil. If[18] only 5 percent of these people actually made pur-

chases, a great deal of money would be involved. When the[19] first supply of oil was sold, it might be replaced with lower-priced oil because of the quick turnover.

When goods are[20] left on the shelves of a store, employees sit idle. The manufacturer of the goods does not have work to do.[21] The sales representatives have no customers, and business cannot progress. When the general public knows[22] about goods that are available, however, suppliers can go ahead and manufacture their products in large[23] quantities and thus effect a lower unit cost. They can actually sell the goods to wholesalers or retailers[24] at lower prices. The wholesalers and retailers can then sell them to the public at lower unit[25] prices.

After a quick review of what advertising actually does for business, it is easy to see that[26] advertising does not cost; it actually pays. Without advertising, business would not be able to get its[27] message across to the public. Advertising is truly a window for business.   [554]

4 Advertising Today

Over the years advertising has become a major function in most businesses. Companies often have[1] advertising departments that work for the entire organization. Some companies are so large, however,[2] that they have an advertising unit within each of the various departments. It is not unusual[3] for an organization that employs 1,000 or 2,000 people to have 40, 50, or more[4] people working to advertise the goods and services that the company produces. The advertising budget[5] for a small company might be $5,000 or $10,000. A large organization might[6] expend as much as $1 million for advertising.

People who work in advertising do not actually[7] produce the goods or services that a company offers to the public. However, it is through their help[8] that these things finally reach the public. If it were not for the work of the people who handle the advertising[9] of a product, the product itself might not succeed in the marketplace. A good, useful item might never[10] be seen by potential customers, and it would eventually have to be taken off the market.

People[11] who write advertising copy are experts in advertising. They are not usually experts in a[12] particular line of goods. They must depend on those who actually make the goods or provide the services[13] to tell them all about the things that are to be sold. Then the advertising staff prepares various types of[14] messages that tell the complete sales story accurately and convincingly.

The message might be used in radio,[15] television, or newspaper advertising. Or it could even be used in circulars, brochures, or[16] personal letters that will be mailed to potential customers. For some items the advertising message must be[17] prepared to reach 5,000 or 10,000 people in one community. For products that are to be sold[18] nationally, the message will have to be de-signed to appeal to perhaps 10 million or 20 million people.[19]

The members of the advertising staff must determine who are the potential buyers of a particular[20] item and try to get the right message to those persons. Defining the potential buyers of goods or services[21] is not ordinarily an easy job. Advertisers must position the products properly if they are to be successful. If the advertising message reaches the wrong people, there will[22] probably be very few sales.

The work of the advertising staff is truly fascinating. A career in[23] this field is for a creative, thoughtful person who can make the right decisions quickly and easily. [478]

CHAPTER 16

LESSON 76

Office-Style Dictation
2 *(As dictated)* Dear Mr. Wilson: Thank you for your letter requesting information about our various types of insurance. We are, of course, very glad to send you the information you need.

We carry health and life insurance (make that *life and health insurance*) for people of all ages. In addition, we carry theft and liability (no, *liability and theft*) insurance for your home.

I am sure, Mr. Wilson, that we will be able to supply you with just the insurance that you need at the price you want to pay.

For more information, just fill out and return the enclosed card.

One of our experienced, well-trained (change that to *well-trained, experienced*) representatives will call on you at your convenience. Sincerely yours,

2 *(As it would be transcribed)*
Dear Mr. Wilson: Thank you for your letter requesting information about our various types of insurance.[1] We are, of course, very glad to send you the information you need.

We carry life and health insurance for[2] people of all ages. In addition, we carry liability and theft insurance for your home.

I am[3] sure, Mr. Wilson, that we will be able to supply you with just the insurance that you need at the price you[4] want to pay.

For more information, just fill out and return the enclosed card. One of our well-trained, experienced[5] representatives will call on you at your convenience. Sincerely yours, [113]

4 Ladies and Gentlemen: I recently sold my home in the suburbs and moved into a cooperative apartment[1] in Denver. While I was living in a one-family home, I carried full fire, theft, and liability[2] insurance. I feel that it would be a good idea to protect myself against the possibility of a[3] lawsuit resulting from personal injury to anyone visiting my apartment.

If you think it would[4] be to my advantage to have liability insurance, I hope you will send me any information[5] you have about this particular type of insurance coverage. Sincerely yours, [115]

5 Dear Miss Gates: This is to acknowledge receipt of your request for information about our liability[1] insurance for your new cooperative apartment. Congratulations on the purchase of your new apartment[2] home.

You are quite right; you certainly will need liability insurance to protect yourself against a[3] possible lawsuit resulting from personal injury to anyone visiting your property. However,[4] you will probably also need insurance on the contents of your apartment. While most cooperative apartments[5] have fire and theft insurance for the building itself, most of these insurance policies do not[6] ordinarily cover personal property and furnishings inside the individual apartments. If you should[7] experience a fire, you might lose all your valuable furniture and personal property. In our[8] opinion, it would definitely be to your advantage to carry fire, theft, and liability insurance.[9]

Take this opportunity to read the enclosed brochure carefully. We will be happy to answer any[10] further questions you may have about insurance. Sincerely yours, [211]

6 Gentlemen: In several months I will be moving to Knoxville, and I would like to inquire about the automobile[1] insurance rates in the city. I plan to live in the suburbs and will usually drive my car to and from[2] work at the General Manufacturing Company in the uptown area. It is, of course, important[3] that I be fully covered in case of accident.

Will you please send me information about insurance rates[4] in Knoxville. Very truly yours, [84]

7 Dear Mr. Davis: The letter you wrote to our New York office several days ago has been forwarded to[1] me. Thank you for calling to our attention the matter of the underpayment of your insurance claim.

I have[2] looked into the matter personally, and I believe I understand the problem. As you stated, your original[3] claim was for $600, the amount estimated by the automobile repair shop. We agreed[4] to pay $500. A check for $300 was sent to you in error; it should have been for[5] $500, of course.

I am, therefore, enclosing another check for an additional $200[6] to make up the difference.

I hope, Mr. Davis, that this will settle the matter to your complete satisfaction.[7] If we can be of service to you in the future, please call us. Sincerely yours,
[155]

8 Dear Mr. Worth: This year the Insurance Club of Eastern State College is hosting the annual state convention[1] of college insurance clubs. We would like to have our main banquet at the Worth Restaurant. Will you please give us an[2] estimate of the cost of having the banquet at your restaurant.

We expect to have about 300 persons[3] at the banquet. We would like to have a salad, a main course, a dessert, and a beverage for each person.[4] We will need a room that has a riser in the front for a head table to accommodate 20 persons. In[5] addition, we will need a piano for after-dinner entertainment.

We would appreciate receiving[6] an estimate of the cost of such a banquet as soon as possible so that we may make our plans definite.[7] Very cordially yours, [144]

9 Dear Ms. Casey: Have you checked your home insurance lately? If you have not, you may be in for a big surprise. In[1] the past few years houses throughout the city have increased in value substantially, and many are dangerously[2] underinsured.

In yesterday's newspaper you probably read about the *tragic** fire that occurred in your[3] neighborhood. Fortunately, the owners of that house, who are covered by our company, had recently brought their[4] insurance coverage up to date.

Take a few minutes to look over your policy now. If your home is worth[5] 20 percent more than the face value of your policy, you should increase your coverage without delay. One of[6] our well-trained, experienced representatives will be *happy†* to talk with you at your convenience. Sincerely[7] yours, [141]
Also correct:
*terrible
†glad, delighted

LESSON 77

5 Dear Mr. Cunningham: Thank you very much for your inquiry about our insurance policies. Your letter[1] arrived at our Camden, New Jersey, office several days ago; however, it just reached my desk today.

I am[2] sending you a copy of our latest brochure describing all the types of insurance that our company[3] offers. I hope you will take a few minutes to look through the book. When you have had an opportunity to do[4] so, please call me so that I may have the opportunity to come to your home at your convenience to discuss[5] these policies with you.

Thank you for your interest in our insurance company, Mr. Cunningham. I hope to[6] hear from you soon. Sincerely yours, [126]

6 Dear Mr. Paterson: I hope you are happy with your new General freezer, which you purchased several days[1] ago. As you know, the freezer is covered by factory warranty for a full one-year period. At this time[2] we would like to offer you the opportunity to purchase extended in-home service for your freezer for[3] an additional one-year period. For only $50 you can extend the contract for an entire[4] year. We will supply both parts and service should you experience any trouble with the appliance.

This extended[5] contract offers unlimited service calls for repairs or replacements at any time. There are no hidden[6] charges, and one of our reliable service representatives will be at your home within a few hours[7] after we receive your call.

To apply for the extended policy, just fill out the enclosed card, attach your check[8] or money order for $50, and mail both to us in the envelope that is provided.

If you would[9] like to have any further information about our extended service policy, you may call us at our[10] Pittsburgh office; our phone number is 555-8020. Sincerely yours, [214]

7 Dear Sir or Madam: On March 1 I purchased a service policy that was to cover any repair costs for[1] my television set for a one-year period. Two weeks ago I began experiencing trouble with[2] the picture on the set. I could not adjust the brightness, and the colors faded after the set had been on for[3] only a few minutes.

I called your company and made an appointment for repairs to be made the following[4] week. I arranged to be in the house all day on July 3, but no one from your company came on that date. At[5] 4 p.m. I called and found that the office was preparing to close early for the holiday on the next day[6] and that all repairs were to have been completed by noon. The dispatcher checked the schedule and told me that I was[7] not on the schedule for the day's work. Needless to say, I was upset. The dispatcher was very nice, and I[8] agreed to make another appointment for July 8.

On that day I received a call at 2 p.m. stating that[9] your company would be unable to get to my house until the next day. I simply could not spend another[10] day waiting for someone who might or might not show up. I had the television set repaired by another[11] company.

I now wish to have my service policy canceled and the premium refunded in full. I expect[12] to hear from you by return mail. Yours truly, [248]

8 Dear Miss Smith: It is not often that we get a letter such as the one you wrote to us on Friday, June[1] 26. Most people take our insurance claim service for granted and write to us only when they receive service that[2] is somewhat less than they expect.

When we do receive a letter like yours, it makes us feel particularly proud[3] to be in the insurance business. We know that we have lived up to our goal of providing quick, efficient, and[4] dependable service.

Thank you, Miss Smith, for taking valuable time from your busy day to write us. Whenever[5] we may be of further service to you in the future, I hope you will let us know. Yours very truly, [118]

9 Dear Ms. Torres: Thank you for using the General credit card for another year. Yes, one more year has passed since[1] you last paid the small annual membership fee of $15. I am *sure** that you have used the card in[2] many ways and in many places during the year. Thank you for your continued confidence in America's most[3] widely used credit card. We are enclosing your statement for the coming year for continuation of this[4] service.

For the first time this year we are including accident insurance as a service to all General[5] credit card holders. Each time you use your General credit card to pay for a plane, train, or bus ticket, you will[6] automatically receive $25,000 worth of life insurance. I hope you will agree, Ms.[7] Torres, that this insurance is one of the best services that we have ever provided for our credit card holders.[8]

Just return the enclosed form with your check, and your new card will be *mailed*† to you within two weeks. Very cordially[9] yours, [181]

Also correct:
*confident
†sent, forwarded

LESSON 78

4 Dear Mr. White: Last week I received your check for $1,000 to cover the loss I incurred when I was[1] involved in a serious automobile accident several months ago. On the bottom of the check was a[2] note stating that it was in full payment.

As you know, Mr. White, the claim amounted to $3,000, which[3] is $2,000 more than the amount you mailed me. If you made the assumption that I would accept this[4] payment, you were totally wrong. I have turned the uncashed check over to my attorney with the instruction to hold it[5] until proper settlement has been made.

Mr. James Edwards, your policyholder, is legally[6] responsible for the accident. My actual bills have been more than $3,000, and I can substantiate[7] this very easily. I will expect a check for the remaining $2,000 immediately. If[8]

I do not receive it by return mail, I will initiate a lawsuit; I have no alternative. Yours[9] truly,   [181]

5 Dear Miss Wright: Thank you for your letter of March 21 concerning your claim against Mrs. Mary Palmer, who[1] holds a policy with our company.

We have discussed the problem at length with Mrs. Palmer, and she assures[2] us that the injury you suffered in the automobile accident on February 20 was[3] totally your responsibility. She explained that you were attempting to pass her car at the intersection[4] of Main and Elm Streets when your car hit an electric light pole. The police officer's report of the accident[5] substantiates this. Therefore, your claim for $1,000 against Mrs. Palmer must be rejected.

We suggest[6] that you write to a representative of your own insurance company. Yours truly,
    [136]

6 Dear Mr. White: Do you remember when you could purchase a postage stamp for only 3 cents? Do you remember[1] when you could buy a candy bar for only 5 cents? Many people do remember those times, but the days of the[2] 3-cent stamp and the 5-cent candy bar are gone forever.

Also gone forever are the days when a hospital[3] room cost $10 or $20 a day. However, many Americans still have hospital[4] insurance that pays such small sums. It seems that over the years people simply forget to look at their insurance[5] policies. They make the assumption that their policies are just as good today as they were when they originally[6] purchased them.

Don't you think it would be a good idea, Mr. White, to take a look at exactly what insurance[7] you have. You might find out that your policy is totally out of date.

If you wish, I will come to your home at[8] your convenience and personally review your entire insurance program. I can plan an effective, up-to-date[9] medical insurance program for you if your current policy is insufficient to meet your needs. Just[10] call me at 555-1472. Please do it right now; you will be under no obligation, of course.[11] Sincerely yours,   [223]

7 Dear Mr. Brown: Do you have a friend or relative who is approaching retirement? If you do, you could do that[1] person a big favor by sending him or her a copy of the enclosed pamphlet. The pamphlet describes our[2] complete hospital, medical, and surgical plans for senior citizens. Our insurance program is designed to[3] supplement Medicare insurance to help older Americans meet the expenses of health care after retirement.[4]

If you want additional copies of the pamphlet, just write to us at 211 West First Avenue[5] in Harrisburg, Pennsylvania. We will appreciate receiving your letter, and we are sure that your friends will[6] appreciate having copies of the pamphlet. Yours truly,   [131]

8 Dear Mrs. Moore: We are happy to announce several major improvements in our company's medical[1] insurance coverage. As a member of the work force here at International Enterprises, you have[2] several new benefits we think you will appreciate. These benefits are effective immediately.

You now[3] have an increase of $20 per day in the amount paid for a hospital room. You also have an[4] increase of 10 percent for each of the operations listed on page 6 of your insurance policy. Finally,[5] you now have an increase in the number of days you may be away from the office with full pay because of[6] illness.

We think this additional coverage is a positive step, and we believe you will agree with us,[7] Mrs. Moore. Sincerely yours,   [145]

9 Dear Mr. Jones: Several weeks ago your insurance premium was due, but we have not yet received your payment.[1] We know, of course, that occasionally a person forgets to put a check in the mail. It could be that your check[2] actually was *lost*† after you mailed it.

It is *extremely*† important to you and to your family that your[3] valuable insurance be kept effective. If your insurance is allowed to lapse, resumption of this service[4] could take as long as six months. In addition, you would have to qualify by taking a new physical[5] examination.

Will you please take a few minutes' time right now to write your check and mail it to us. Sincerely yours,   [119]

Also correct:
*misplaced
†very

4 Dear Dave: I was disappointed to learn that you have not been able to hire Tom Washington to represent our[1] insurance company in the state of Texas. I did everything in my power to encourage Tom to[2] accept the position, but he was quite reluctant to leave California, where his parents live.

I do, however,[3] have another person to recommend for the position. Her name is June Mason, and she already lives in[4] Texas. Therefore, she would not have to move away from her present home. I have found June to be a person of[5] dependability, integrity, and sincerity. In addition, she has held a prominent position[6] with a major insurance company for the past three years.

I hope that she will accept a permanent position[7] with our company. Her full name, address, and telephone number are shown on the enclosed card; please get in touch[8] with her immediately. May Torres   [167]

5 Dear Miss Hamilton: Mrs. Martha Cummings, who formerly worked for your insurance company, has applied for[1] a position as a corresponding secretary with the General Insurance Company of New[2] Mexico. She gave us your name and stated that you would be able to tell us anything we needed to know[3] about her work.

Would you be good enough to fill out the enclosed form to let us know your opinion of Mrs.[4] Cummings. We are particularly interested in hiring a person with personal integrity and[5] maturity of judgment. Any information you can give us will be sincerely appreciated.

If we[6] can ever be of similar service to your company, we will be happy to help you. Yours truly,   [138]

6 Dear Mr. Harding: Your letter asking for a reference for Mr. Calvin Jones arrived in this morning's mail.[1]

Mr. Jones worked for my company only a short period of time, and he was not under my direct[2] supervision. I asked several of his associates to give me a general description of his attitude and[3] ability. None of the people who worked with him were able to give me much information. However, they[4] did not seem to have been disappointed with his work.

I can tell you that Mr. Jones was on our payroll for less[5] than one year and left about six months ago to accept a permanent position on the faculty of the[6] Lexington School of Insurance. Perhaps someone at that school could supply you with more information about his[7] ability. Sincerely yours,   [146]

7 Dear Miss Smith: Thank you very much for the nice letter of recommendation you wrote for me last week. Thanks also[1] for *sending** me a copy of the letter. I am happy to tell you that I have accepted a permanent[2] position on the faculty of Birmingham College. I will be teaching several courses in insurance[3] beginning with the fall term.

If you are in the Birmingham area in the near future, I hope you will come to[4] the college for a visit. It would be *wonderful*† to see you again, Miss Smith. Sincerely yours,   [97]
Also correct:
*mailing
†nice

LESSON 80

3 *The Value of Insurance*

If you ever apply for a large loan from a commercial bank, a savings bank, or[1] other lending organization, you will probably be asked to list the value of each of your assets. You[2] will be asked to give the current value of your house, your automobile, and any property you may[3] own. In addition, you will probably be asked to state the amount of life insurance you own.

Many people[4] never really think of life insurance as an asset, but it actually is. If you have permanent life[5] insurance, it probably has a substantial face value that would be paid to your beneficiaries if[6] you should die. The policy might also have a paid-up cash value, which you may redeem at any time. It might[7] also have value as collateral if you should wish to pledge the policy to guarantee a loan you want[8] to make. You might wish to borrow against the policy to pay a tax bill, to finance a car, or to make some[9] type of large purchase. It is easy to see that life insurance has real monetary value and should be[10] treated as an actual asset.

But life insurance has other types of value also. Insurance provides peace[11] of mind for you and your family. If you are responsible for a spouse and several small children, you can relax[12] in the knowledge that if you should die, your family could maintain their current style of life without having to move[13] to a less expensive neighborhood or rely on friends or relatives for support. This peace of mind is worth a[14] great amount to most people.

Health insurance also has value. If you become ill and have to undergo a[15] major operation, health insurance could help you pay doctors' bills, hospital bills, and the cost of medication.[16] Should you have to stay in the hospital from November to January, for example, your bills could well[17] be enough to deplete your family's entire savings. With health insurance most of these bills would be paid, and your[18] savings would remain in the bank.

Another type of insurance that many people feel is of extreme value[19] is salary-continuation insurance. If the breadwinner of a family becomes ill and cannot[20] work for several months, his or her salary would continue as usual with this type of insurance.

One[21] other type of insurance, which is similar to salary-continuation insurance, is disability[22] insurance. This type of insurance ordinarily pays a fixed amount per month to a person who is[23] unable to work. With disability insurance there may be a waiting period of perhaps two or[24] three months before payments begin. For example, if an employee becomes ill or is injured and cannot work[25] in October, disability insurance might begin paying in December or January. It would[26] continue as long as the person is unable to work or until the terms of the policy expire.[27]

Another type of insurance that is particularly valuable to young persons is mortgage redemption[28] insurance. If the breadwinner of a young family buys a home, he or she might take out this type of insurance.[29] Mortgage redemption insurance is, of course, a type of life insurance. If the person dies, the remaining[30] amount due on the mortgage is paid. This protects the family members by giving them a house free of debt at[31] a time that is both emotionally and economically taxing.

It is easy to see that insurance[32] has value in many ways.   [646]

4 How Insurance Companies Operate

How can insurance companies stay in business? When you first think about the insurance business, it might seem that[1] it would be very difficult for the average company to operate successfully. Most people pay[2] only a small monthly, quarterly, or annual fee for their insurance coverage. Yet when they have a claim,[3] it usually amounts to much more than they have paid in total premiums during the year.

If this is true,[4] how can any insurance company make enough money to be successful? The answer to that question lies[5] in what are generally called risk tables. These tables are prepared by individual insurance companies,[6] insurance associations, or the industry as a whole.

Actuaries keep records for many years[7] to determine just what the probability is that a particular person will have an insurance claim.[8] Persons are assigned to certain risk categories. Several of the things that are considered include the age[9] of the person, where and under what conditions the person works, and the person's medical history. When the[10] records of all people are compiled, the insurance company decides just what it must charge a person in each[11] category. The total premiums must be large enough to pay for any claims made by anyone in the[12] category and still ensure a reasonable profit for the insurance company. The company is[13] not looking at only one person's record; it is looking at all people in a particular classification.[14] The risk tables are revised continuously and kept up to date. If experience shows that a[15] certain category is having increasingly higher claims, the premiums for the group will be increased. On the[16] other hand, a group may be identified for which the premiums can be lowered significantly.[17] Insurance companies are quite eager to establish lower premiums whenever possible in order to[18] attract new business.

Insurance companies are generally regulated by agencies of the government.[19] This is to ensure that all policyholders are treated fairly. However, the real regulation comes in[20] the form of competition. One insurance company might have to charge more for the same coverage than[21] another simply because it costs more to manage and operate that particular company. Policyholders[22] should always compare the cost of similar coverage with at least two or three companies before deciding[23] where to buy insurance.

Over the years the average person is not likely to have claims that amount to more[24] than the premiums which that particular person has paid. Each year part of that person's premium goes to help pay[25] the administrative costs of the company. Part of it goes to help pay the claims of others who[26] actually did suffer losses. And part of the premium goes to provide a dividend for those who own stock in[27] the company.

Insurance companies help individuals to prepare for possible losses by spreading[28] the risk among thousands of people. In this way the individual is protected, and the insurance[29] company can stay in business and operate successfully.   [592]

APPENDIX

RECALL DRILLS

Joined Word Endings
1   Treatment, alignment, supplement, amusement, compliment, experiment.
2   Nation, termination, station,

operation, inflation, relation, caution, portion, section, promotion.

3 Credential, confidential, essential, commercial, socially.

4 Greatly, namely, nicely, mainly, nearly, highly, only, properly, surely, mostly.

5 Readily, speedily, easily, hastily, necessarily, family.

6 Careful, thoughtful, delightful, mindful, usefulness, awful, helpful, powerful, respectful, faithful.

7 Dependable, reliable, profitable, table, troubled.

8 Gather, gathered, together, rather, either, leather, bother, bothered, neither, mother.

9 Actual, actually, gradual, schedule, annual, equally.

10 Furniture, picture, nature, stature, captured, miniature, failure, natural, feature.

11 Yourself, myself, itself, himself, herself, themselves, ourselves, yourselves.

12 Port, sport, import, report, deportment.

13 Contain, retain, certain, container, contained.

14 Efficient, sufficient, deficient, efficiency, deficiency, proficiency.

Disjoined Word Endings
15 Childhood, motherhood, neighborhood, brotherhood.

16 Forward, backward, onward, afterward, rewarded.

17 Relationship, steamship, authorship, professorship, championship.

18 Radical, technical, political, article, chemically, periodically, logically, practically.

19 Congratulate, regulate, stipulates, tabulated, congratulation, regulation, regulations, stipulations.

20 Willingly, exceedingly, knowingly, surprisingly, grudgingly.

21 Readings, mornings, sidings, dressings, savings, drawings, sayings, blessings, feelings, servings.

22 Program, telegram, telegrams, diagrams.

23 Notification, modification, specifications, classifications, ratification.

24 Personality, ability, reliability, facilities, utility, generalities, locality.

25 Faculty, penalty, casualty, loyalty.

26 Authority, sincerity, majority, minority, clarity, sorority, charity, seniority.

Joined Word Beginnings
27 Permit, perform, perfect, pertain, persist, purchase, pursue, pursued, purple, purse.

28 Employ, empower, embarrass, embody, empire, emphatic, embrace, emphasis, emphasize.

29 Impress, impression, imply, impossible, impair, impel, imbue, impact, imperfect.

30 Increase, intend, income, inform, inconsistent, indeed, inference, inferior, insane, inscribe.

31 Enlarge, enforce, enlist, encourage, enjoy, enrich, encounter, encircle, enrage.

32 Unkind, unwritten, unwilling, unsuccessful, undo, unpleasant, untie, unpopular.

33 Refer, resign, receive, reform, reorganize.

34 Beneath, believe, belong, before, became.

35 Delay, deliver, deserve, diligent.

36 Dismiss, disappoint, discover, discuss, despite.
37 Mistake, misquote, misspell, misstate, misunderstand, misapplied, mistrust.
38 Explain, excite, extend, excuse, express, exit.
39 Comprise, comfort, comply, completed, compete.
40 Condition, consult, continue, confident, convey, confess.
41 Submit, substantiate, subdivide, sublease, suburban.
42 Almost, also, already, although, alteration.
43 Forget, forceful, performed, forecast, foreman.
44 Furnish, furnished, furnishings, furniture, furnace, further, furtive.
45 Turn, turned, term, attorney, determine, eastern.
46 Ultimate, ulterior, adult, culture, result.

Disjoined Word Beginnings
47 Interested, internal, interview, intercept, introduce, entrance, entrances, introduction, enterprise, entertain, entered.
48 Electricity, electrician, electrical, electric wire, electric fan, electric light, electric motor, electrode.
49 Supervise, supervision, supervisor, superhuman, superb, superior.
50 Circumstance, circumstances, circumstantial, circumvent, circumspect.
51 Selfish, self-made, self-defense, self-respect, self-conscious, self-assured.
52 Transit, transfer, transact, transplant, translation.
53 Understand, undertake, undergo, underpaid, undermine, understate, underline, underscore, understood, undercover.
54 Overcome, overdue, overhead, overture, overpay, oversee, overdraw, overgrow, overlook, overnight, oversight.

Key to Chart on Page 447

Brief Forms of Gregg Shorthand in Alphabetical Order

1 A-an, about, acknowledge, advantage, advertise, after, am.
2 And, any, are-our-hour, be-by, business, but, can.
3 Character, characters, circular, company, correspond-correspondence, corresponded, could.
4 Difficult, doctor, enclose, envelope, every-ever, executive, experience.
5 For, from, general, gentlemen, glad, good, govern.
6 Government, have, I, idea, immediate, important-importance, in-not.
7 Is-his, it-at, manufacture, morning, Mr., Mrs., Ms.
8 Never, newspaper, next, object, objected, of, one (won).
9 Opinion, opportunity, order, ordinary, organize, out, over.
10 Part, particular, present, probable, progress, public, publish-publication.
11 Quantity, question, recognize, regard, regular, request, responsible.
12 Satisfy-satisfactory, send, several, short, should, soon, speak.

13 State, street, subject, success, suggest, than, thank.

14 That, the, them, there (their), they, thing-think, this.

15 Throughout, time, under, usual, value, very, was.

16 Were, what, when, where, which, will-well, wish.

17 With, work, world, worth, would, yesterday, you-your.

Transcript of Page 121

How Big Should My Shorthand Be?

Each writer must set his own size for his shorthand writing. Whatever size seems right to you is probably the best[1] size for you. One skillful shorthand reporter writes 500 words of shorthand on an ordinary notebook page;[2] another writes only 50 words on a similar page. Neither extreme is recommended. If you naturally[3] find yourself writing very large notes or very small notes, you need not be concerned about the size of your notes.[4]

If you write whatever size of shorthand notes seems to be natural for you, the size will have little or no effect[5] on your speed. If you try constantly to write notes larger or smaller than you would naturally write, you may[6] find that the attempt to change the size of your notes hinders the development of your speed.

[132]—*Martin J. Dupraw*